arnold's fitness for kids

ages 11–14

doubleday

new york

london

toronto

sydney

auckland

arnold's fitness for kids

ages 11–14
a guide to health, exercise, and nutrition

arnold schwarzenegger
with charles gaines

illustrations by jackie aher and denise donnell

Finished art assisted by Douglas Reinke

published by doubleday

a division of Bantam Doubleday Dell Publishing Group, Inc.
666 Fifth Avenue, New York, New York 10103

doubleday and the portrayal of an anchor with a
dolphin are trademarks of Doubleday, a division of
Bantam Doubleday Dell Publishing Group, Inc.

Book design by Marysarah Quinn and Claire N. Vaccaro
Handlettering, endpaper, and illustration on page 54 by
Robert de Michiell

Library of Congress Cataloging-in-Publication Data

Schwarzenegger, Arnold.
  [Fitness for kids ages 11–14]
  Arnold's fitness for kids ages 11–14 : a guide to health, exercise, and
nutrition / Arnold Schwarzenegger with Charles Gaines.—1st ed.
    p.   cm.
  Includes bibliographical references.
  Summary: A guide to physical fitness for adolescents, with activities
and stories related to health, exercise, and nutrition.
1. Physical fitness for children—Juvenile literature.   [1. Physical
fitness.   2. Exercise.
3. Nutrition.]   I. Gaines, Charles, 1942–   II. Title.
GV443.S384   1993
613.7′042–dc20   92-26786
                                                  CIP
                                                  AC

ISBN 0-385-42268-7

To my parents Gustav and
Aurelia, who instilled in me
that priceless gift, the
lifelong love of sports,
exercise, and pride
in striving for excellence.
Their love, support, and
encouragement are the
foundation of my life.
—Arnold Schwarzenegger

This series is also dedicated
to the world's children with
the wish that we could give
every one of them the
priceless gift of lifelong
fitness and good health.
—Arnold Schwarzenegger
and Charles Gaines

Contents

INTRODUCTION

a note to parents from arnold

This is a book on fitness and good health for kids ages eleven through fourteen. It defines the term fitness and explains why it is so crucially important to their present and future lives. It tells kids in terms they can understand what fitness means to health and how it adds to performance and to the enjoyment of life. It also shows them how they can construct customized fitness programs for themselves, tells them how to eat "smart," and discusses sports participation and physical education in their schools.

Your child can use this book to get and stay fit, and to develop habits of exercise and good nutrition that can lead to a lifetime of vigor and good health—*but not without your help*. Later in this Introduction, I'll tell you exactly what you can do to help your child make the best possible use of this book. But first, let's look at why he or she *needs* to make use of it.

As I travel around the country in my position as chairman of the President's Council on Physical Fitness and Sports, I am constantly amazed by how little parents are concerned about the fitness levels of their children, and by the general lack of information available on the significance of the youth fitness crisis in this country. The facts that underlie and define that crisis are: (1) *the great majority of American kids are physically unfit;* (2) *those kids are on a fast track to becoming unhealthy adults;* and (3) *the situation is getting worse rather than better.* As my friend Dr. Kenneth Cooper has summed it up in his book *Kid Fitness,* "Millions of our children

—the majority of them in middle- and upper-middle-class homes—face the prospect of serious disease and shortened life spans because of sedentary living and poor nutrition."

One of the questions I hear surprisingly often from parents is, "We know why it's important for Billy to get a good education, but why is it so important for him to be physically fit?" The answer is, simply, that both the length and the quality of Billy's life depend on it.

Fitness, after all, is just another word for good health, and chances are that unfit kids are less healthy than fit ones. As Bob Glover and Jack Shepherd write in *The Family Fitness Handbook,* "Kids who are physically fit are at lower risk for hypokinetic diseases such as hypertension, cardiovascular disease, tension syndromes, diabetes, gastrointestinal disease (ulcers—yes, our high-stressed kids get ulcers), and emotional problems. *These degenerative diseases all begin in childhood."* (Italics mine.)

Of the potential health liabilities of poor fitness among kids, the most serious is heart disease, which is the leading cause of death and disability in America. If you think heart disease has nothing to do with childhood, think again. According to *The Research Quarterly,* "It is well established that atherosclerotic heart disease begins at an early age and available evidence suggests that physical activity in children is inversely associated with other coronary risk factors." And Dr. Elvin Smith of the Texas A&M College of Medicine writes, "Much of heart disease can be traced to having its initiation in early childhood. If nothing more is done, we'll continue to see a gradual slip in fitness and kids will have a difficult time making any impact on heart disease. It makes little sense to invest in a child's education and leave him at risk for heart disease."

But maybe you are one of those nine out of ten parents who thinks that risk doesn't apply to you because your kid is in great shape and gets plenty of exercise. The chances are excellent that you're dead wrong. The fact is that kids across the board are fatter and less fit than they were fifteen years ago, including, very possibly, your own. Just look at a few of these statistics:

▶ Obesity among children twelve to seventeen has increased 39 percent since the 1960s, according to a 1987 study conducted by the Harvard School of Public Health.

▶ A University of Michigan study showed that 50 percent of all American kids in kindergarten through twelfth grade have at least one risk factor for heart disease.

▶ One third of all youths ages ten to eighteen don't engage in enough physical activity to give them *any* aerobic or endurance benefit, according to the 1987 National Children and Youth Fitness Study.

▶ Only *one* state, Illinois, has a mandatory daily physical education requirement for all students, kindergarten through high school.

▶ Only 32 percent of children ages six to seventeen meet *minimum* standards for cardiovascular fitness, flexibility, and abdominal and upper-body strength, according to a 1989 AAU study of twelve thousand youths. (In 1981, 43 percent of the children were in acceptable shape.)

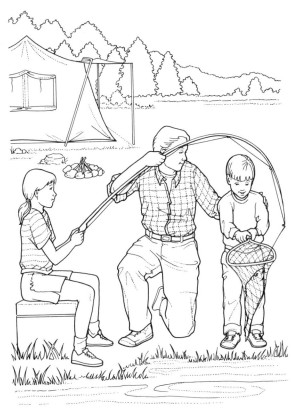

▶ In 1979–80, 57 percent of four million American kids ages six to seventeen failed to meet the AAU's fitness standard for an "average healthy youngster"; in a follow-up study in 1984, that number had risen to 64 percent, and by 1987, the fitness failure rate among nine million American kids had reached a shocking 71 percent.

We've been going *backward!*

That's the bad news. But here's the good news: the downward trend in youth fitness *can* be turned around—one American household at a time, with parents and kids working together in a "fit kid" partnership. The benefits for your child from such a partnership are enormous, and include much more than just extended good health. Fit kids are happier kids. They have better posture, sleep and move better, recover more quickly from sickness and injury, have more endurance and concentration, and can handle physical emergencies more easily than unfit kids. As you will learn in this book, exercise plays a key role in helping young people develop important motor skills such as agility, coordination, and balance. Exercise also helps keep fat off of kids, improving health and making movement easier and more efficient. I have always felt that exercise is tremendously important in boosting self-esteem among young people, and recent studies by child fitness expert Dr. Charles Kuntzleman and others bear this out. When I was a kid, exercise made me feel great about myself. And finally, but by no means least, there's considerable evidence—including a six-year Canadian study—showing that exercise improves academic performance.

Let me ask you this: if there was something you could go out and buy for your child that would make him far healthier, happier, and better prepared to deal with life than he would be without this thing, wouldn't you sell whatever you had to sell, do whatever you had to do, to get it? Well, there is such a thing—fitness. You can't buy it, but you can help your child use this book to put himself or herself onto a lifetime track of fitness and good health—and that may well be the most valuable gift you ever give that child.

how to help your child get the most out of this book

This is not a fitness textbook, full of charts and tables and medical terms, written for teachers, parents, and coaches. As I said earlier, this is a book for kids, addressed *to* them and designed to be used by them. *Arnold's Fitness for Kids Ages Birth–5* addresses the parents of infants, toddlers, and preschoolers and tells them how to give their kids a headstart on fitness by encouraging a love of movement and the development of skills starting from birth. *Arnold's Fitness for Kids Ages 6–10* is addressed to kids ages six through ten and their parents, and deals with how to initiate a family fitness program in the home. This book is addressed directly to the kids themselves (though it enlists parents' help and cannot succeed without that help), because kids eleven through fourteen years old should begin taking responsibility for their own physical well-being, and should begin learning firsthand what they need to know in order to take on that responsibility. To help personalize this book and create a dialogue with the kids reading it, I have included in it a series of stories about myself as an adolescent growing up in Austria, living an energetic, physically active life with my family and friends.

Chapter 1 is a discussion of what fitness is and how it applies to kids in this age range. I discuss the significance of each of the categories of health-related fitness—aerobic, or heart/lung, endurance capacity; flexibility; muscular strength and stamina; and body-fat percentage —and explain how each is relevant to kids ages eleven through fourteen. Finally, I discuss the importance of "motor," or physical, skills, such as balance, agility, and coordination. These skills not only are a prerequisite for performing well at sports, but provide kids with a good "movement base" from which they can effectively take up a wide range of fitness and recreational activities throughout their lives. I encourage you to read and refer to this chapter. There is good, simply stated information on how the body works and on the relationship of different kinds of exercise to good health and good performance.

Chapter 2 explains to your child how to put together his or her own customized fitness program from pretested exercises given in the book's appendixes, and tells him or her how to do those exercises safely and productively. Again, I suggest you read this material yourself, and then help your child design his or her program according to the instructions given in this chapter.

Chapter 3 is a guide to smart and healthful eating, and Chapter 4 takes a look at school physical education programs and sports participation. You will help your child make the best use of this book by reading these chapters as well. (You may have noticed, I have now recommended you read the entire book . . . Arnold, you sneaky devil!)

Here are some other suggestions for helping your child get the most possible benefit from this book.

► Do physical activities and exercises, including the ones recommended here, *with* your child as often as possible. Numerous studies have shown that a child's involvement in physical activity and exercise is heavily influenced by the amount of time his parents spend exercising and doing physical activities with him. You and your child should pick a mutually convenient time of day and give it over to exercising together as often as you possibly can.

► Be a good fitness role model. As child and adolescent psychiatrist Dr. Paul H. Gabriel writes, "The main reason children are out of shape is that they have poor role models. By making fitness a part of your life, you teach your child to value it." What you do or don't do *counts* with your kids, particularly with adolescents. It is almost impossible to convince children not to drink or smoke if you do those things yourself. Similarly, you'll be much more successful in getting your child to exercise regularly if he sees you doing it and enjoying it.

► Provide your child with a good place in your home to exercise—a room, or part of a room, that is large enough and well ventilated—and with an outdoor place as well (if you don't have a suitable backyard, help him locate a safe, convenient park or playground).

► Encourage your child to make exercise a normal, enjoyable, and necessary part of his life. The more varied his physical activity and exercise interests become, the better. Encourage him to try out as many of the lifetime fitness sports as possible (and do them with him). Biking, running, swimming, cross-country skiing, tennis, skating, rowing, etc., can all become great lifelong habits that help make staying in shape fun rather than work. Also encourage your child to try out community classes in dance, yoga, gymnastics, the martial arts, and so on.

► Help your child set realistic and realizable fitness goals for herself and then help her achieve them. One child's goal might be to do five pull-ups by June; another's, to run a sub-eight-minute mile; another's, to lose five pounds. Achieving goals is another way of keeping fitness fun; but keep them realistic—don't try for too much too soon.

▶ Limit your family TV watching. Television robs the entire family of time you could be spending together talking or playing or exercising. In my family we limit TV time to five hours a week, and we all choose together what those five hours will be.

▶ Don't believe, or let your child believe, that school or community-organized team sports programs can substitute for the kind of regular, health-related exercise recommended in this book. In *many* schools and community sports programs, some kids get virtually no exercise, and often what exercise kids do get in team sports offers few fitness benefits.

▶ Learn as much as you can about your child's school physical education program. (See Chapter 4 for how to evaluate it.) If you decide it is deficient, you might want to lobby, perhaps with other parents, to have it improved. Also, find out what the school lunch program is. If it is not as good as it should be, help your child "brown bag" a nutritious lunch from home two or three days a week.

▶ Speaking of food, make smart eating a part of your family life *now*. Set a family "splurge" limit on fast-food meals—two or three a week is plenty.

▶ Make your family vacations active ones. Canoe trips, biking adventures, hiking or climbing expeditions, and cross-country skiing tours make great family vacations. Or go to a family resort where there is a wide range of sports and exercise options, and try them all.

▶ Your child should see your family doctor or pediatrician before beginning an exercise program, particularly if he or she is overweight.

▶ Finally, puberty is an extremely complex time, both physically and emotionally, for your boy or girl, and you should learn as much as you can about it in order to help your child during these years. The use of drugs and alcohol and tobacco, stress, sexually transmitted diseases, pregnancy and suicide, are all physical and emotional dangers that suddenly threaten our kids, usually beginning around the time of puberty. The average amount of time American parents spend with their teenage children is ten to twenty minutes a day—which means that most kids are going through the most confusing and tumultuous period of their lives essentially alone and unguided! The fitness practices recommended in this or any other book have to be based on good health habits that originate in the home. Teenagers, for example, should *never* skip breakfast, and yet half of all American teenage girls, and one third of teenage boys, do not eat breakfast regularly, according to the 1988 National Adolescent Student Health Survey. Adolescents need about nine hours of sleep a night to function at their best, and yet few get that. Learn how to address these issues with your child, and make sure you spend enough time with your adolescent to give him or her the emotional security he or she needs. Also work at providing him or her with a solid foundation of good health and exercise habits that will make the process of getting and staying fit an easy and natural one.

More kids drop out of sports and quit exercising between ages eleven and fifteen than at any other time. There are many reasons for this. Boys who are a little late in entering puberty often find they can no longer compete physically with boys who may be the same age but who have already begun the spurt in growth and strength and speed that comes with the onset of puberty. Unfortunately, these less physically developed boys often retire to the sidelines, literally and figuratively, of exercise and sports participation, sometimes for life. Girls, who normally enter puberty two years before boys (at about ten or eleven), can exercise and play sports with them on an equal footing (and during their two years' headstart on puberty, often actually have an advantage) until twelve or thirteen, when boys quickly catch up to and then pass them in size, speed, and strength. When this happens, many girls go to the sidelines for good, too. Adolescence is a time of extreme self-consciousness and rigorous social comparison, and many more kids of both sexes head for the sidelines out of embarrassment when they: (1) are cut from sports programs; (2) *think* they are going to be cut from sports programs; and (3) don't perform as well or "look as good" at sports or exercise as some of their peers.

On the other hand, if kids acquire or continue good exercise and nutrition habits in these crucial puberty and early teen years, they are very likely to internalize those habits and carry them into the rest of their lives. In effect, these are the "use it or lose it" years. This book gives your child everything he or she needs to know to "use it"—to get on the track to lifelong fitness and good health. I am counting on you to do everything you can to help him or her get onto that track and stay there. Too many American kids have already "lost it."

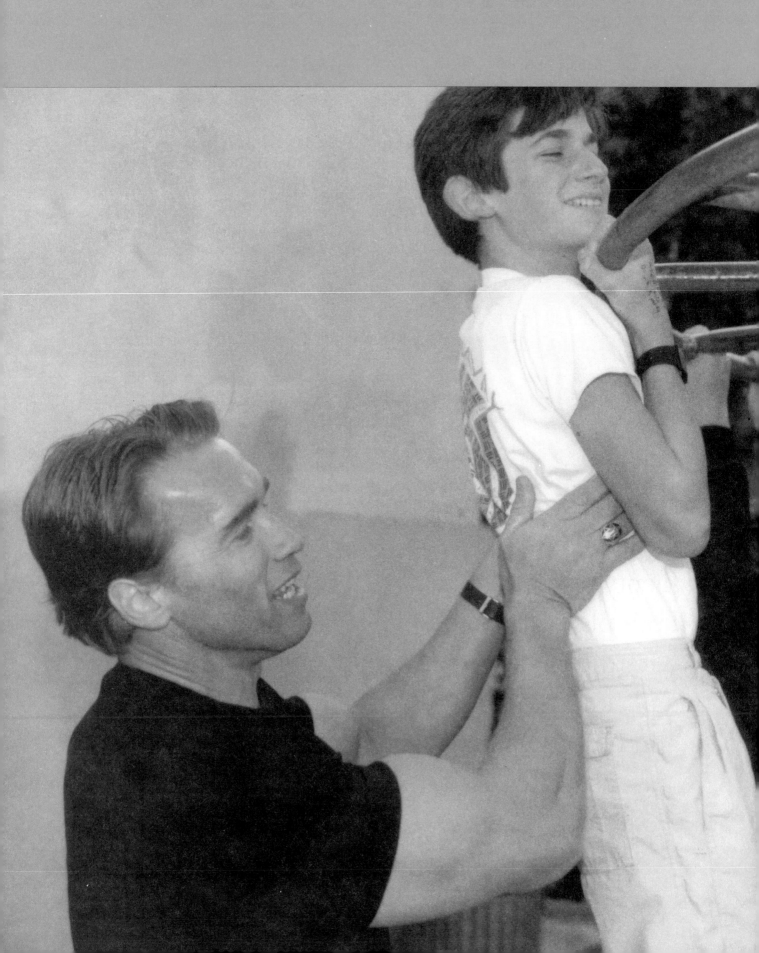

Fitness

1 what is physical fitness and why should you be physically fit?

Back in Austria when I was growing up, *everyone* was physically fit, kids and adults alike. We ate good, healthful, homemade food and got plenty of exercise as a normal part of our lives, both playing and working. Kids played outside with their parents after supper, and went hiking and skiing with them on the weekends, and being in good physical shape was just a natural result of the life we lived.

Unfortunately, most of us don't live like that anymore. Today, in America, we drive everywhere in cars, we don't do much physical work, we watch too much TV, and we eat foods that are not always good for us. For these reasons and others, many Americans of all ages are no longer physically fit, including *most* American young people—people your age. That is a major problem, and one I am working hard to change.

Why is it a problem? Because physical fitness is the same thing as good health. People who are not fit are not as healthy as they should be, and young people who are not fit are likely to become unhealthy adults and likely not to live as long as they should. The future of this great country of ours *depends* on its young people; it depends on as many of you as possible growing up healthy and leading long, productive lives, and that's what I want for each and every one of you.

I have written this book with my friend Charles Gaines to make you aware of how important it is that you become physically fit and stay that way, and to make you aware of how many good things, in addition to health, fitness can bring into your life. If I could wave a magic wand and suddenly make all of you fit for life, I would do it. So would your parents and your teachers, and everyone else who cares about you. But nobody can do that for you. Your body and your health are *your* responsibility, and you are old enough now to take on that responsibility. That's why this book is written to *you*, not to your parents or teachers. If you do the things this book tells you how to do, *you* can make yourself and keep yourself physically fit, and lifetime physical fitness is a backyard full of treasures—every time you turn around, you find a new one.

Let's look now at what some of those treasures are.

An organization called American Alliance of Health, Physical Education, Recreation and Dance (AAHPERD) defines physical fitness as: *"A physical state of well-being that allows people to perform daily activities with vigor, reduce their risk of health problems related to lack of exercise, and to establish a fitness base for participation in a variety of physical activities."*

That's a good definition. But what does it mean for *you?*

▶ First of all, the definition says that fitness is a "state of well-being." That means that you feel good when you're fit—that you're happy—and I can tell you for a fact that I am happy and feel good all the time because I'm fit.

▶ Second, the definition says that being fit lets you "perform daily activities with vigor." That simply means you have more energy for school and play and all the other things you do in your life. It means you move through life more efficiently and more easily and with more endurance and snap. You move through life like a sports car when you're fit, as opposed to a clunky old truck when you're not.

▶ Next, according to the definition, fitness reduces your "risk of health problems related to lack of exercise." If you are fit, in other words, you are less likely to get sick, both while you're young and when you get older. Lack of exercise and eating the wrong foods can cause diabetes, a stroke, high blood pressure, cancer, and heart disease, the last of which is the leading cause of death in America. Some of these diseases, including heart disease, can begin in childhood, so the sooner you start getting fit to avoid them, the better.

▶ And finally, the definition says that fitness lets you establish a "base for participation in a variety of physical activities." That means that when you are fit you are prepared to learn to do a lot of fun things with your body, and to do them well. You do everything of a physical nature, from sports to dancing, better when you're fit. And when you do things well with your body, it builds your self-esteem and you feel good about yourself.

▶ There are other benefits to fitness that this definition doesn't mention. When you are fit, you sleep better, digest your food better, and have a better appetite. You don't get as depressed or anxious when you're fit, and stress doesn't bother you as much. Your posture is better, and your body *looks* better, both to yourself and to other people. And last but not least, you concentrate and *think* better when you are fit, and a number of studies have shown that kids do better in school when they are fit.

▶ So, as you can see, fitness really is a backyard full of treasures. And with a little work, you can make it *your* backyard.

fitness for good health

You can be "physically fit" for a lot of different things. You can be physically fit to sit in a chair all day, but that doesn't mean you're physically fit to climb a mountain. You can be physically fit to hit a baseball a long way, but then have to huff and puff your way around the bases because you're not physically fit for running.

What I care about most is that you are physically fit *to be healthy*. We call that kind of fitness "health-related physical fitness," and there are four parts to it. To be physically fit for good health:

1. Your heart and lungs should be strong and efficient.

2. Your joints and muscles should be flexible.

3. Your muscles should be strong and have endurance.

4. You shouldn't be overly fat.

Now let's take a look at each of those four parts, and see what it has to do with your health.

heart/lung strength

As you probably already know, your heart is a muscle—the most important one in your body —that works all the time pumping blood through your body. The normal heart "beats," or contracts, about one hundred thousand times a day, pumping more than a gallon of blood per minute through thousands of miles of arteries and veins. And that's just when the heart is taking it easy! When you are exercising, it can beat more than twice as fast and can pump *five or six times* more blood. Like any muscle, the heart loves to work, and it gets bigger and stronger (and healthier) with the right kind of exercise.

The right kind of exercise for the heart is called "aerobic," which means exercise that requires a lot of oxygen from the body over an extended time and that improves the body's ability to handle and transport oxygen.

All muscles need oxygen to work, or exercise, and the harder they work, the more oxygen they need. The muscles get oxygen like this: every time you take a breath, air is drawn into millions of little air sacs in the lungs. Those little air sacs load oxygen onto the red blood cells as your blood courses through the wall of each sac. You can think of the sacs as loading depots,

Oxygen

Heart

Lungs

Oxygen carried to the muscles via red blood cells

and the red blood cells as train cars picking up the oxygen in the sacs and carrying it to your muscles. As a muscle or group of muscles begins to work, or exercise, it needs more oxygen than usual and the body supplies that extra oxygen in two ways: the lungs begin to draw in more air, sending more oxygen into the air sacs for delivery, and the heart begins to pump faster, sending more blood through the lungs. With the lungs and the heart both working harder, there is more oxygen in the depots ready for delivery, and more train cars going

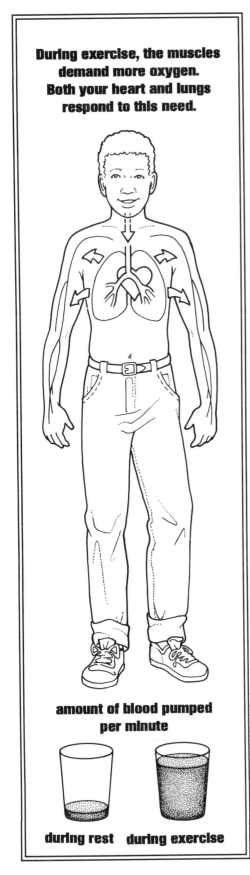

During exercise, the muscles demand more oxygen. Both your heart and lungs respond to this need.

amount of blood pumped per minute

during rest   **during exercise**

through the depots to pick up the oxygen for delivery to the muscles. The next time you're exercising, when your heart begins to beat faster and you start to pant, think of how your heart and lungs are working together to load oxygen and hurry it to your muscles.

The more your heart and lungs and bloody-carrying system work together in this way, the better able they are to do it, and the healthier they are. Also, research shows that regular exercise that forces your heart and lungs to work hard together over a period of time (aerobic exercise) can help you avoid heart disease, as well as many other ailments.

There are many kinds of exercise that help strengthen your heart and lungs and make them work better together. Some of those exercises are brisk walking, running, biking, swimming, cross-country skiing, rowing, jumping rope, and aerobic dance. In the next chapter, I'll talk more about those exercises, and in Appendix A of this book is a list of them for you to choose from in putting together your fitness program.

joint and muscle flexibility

Flexibility is the ability to move your muscles and joints smoothly and fully. Every joint—such as the elbow, knee, back, and hip—has an ideal "range of motion." If your knee, for example, can move smoothly throughout its entire range of motion, it has good flexibility. If it can only move through part of its range of motion, your knee's flexibility is not as good as it should be.

Flexible joints and muscles are less prone to injury than stiff ones, and that is why

they are healthier. Think about it this way: flexible joints and muscles are like strands of cooked spaghetti —you can twist and turn and fold them without breaking or tearing them. Stiff muscles and joints are more like *uncooked* pieces of spaghetti—you can't bend them much without damaging them. Many, many adult Americans have lower-back pain, and often that pain is a result of the back not being flexible enough.

Flexibility not only helps prevent injury, but it also allows you to do many things more easily and better, including a lot of sports, such as gymnastics, swimming, tennis, and skateboarding. Dancers have to be very flexible, too. Good flexibility in all your joints and muscles allows you to move your body easily, gracefully, and injury-free through hundreds of activities.

Most of us are born with very good flexibility in our joints and muscles, but we lose some of that flexibility as we get older. Kids your age are already losing flexibility in both muscles and joints, and the best way to stop that loss is with the right kind of exercise. Stretching is the type of exercise we use to keep muscles and joints flexible, as well as to warm up for aerobic exercise and to cool down after it. In the next chapter, I will tell you more about how and when to do stretching exercises, and at the end of the book, I'll show you a number of good stretches to use in your exercise program.

muscle strength and endurance

Everybody knows that it is better to have strong muscles than weak ones—and that goes for *girls* as well as boys. It is also *healthier* to have strong muscles, because they are like the body's armor protecting us from injury. Strong muscles can also prevent people from developing back, neck, and other problems. Despite

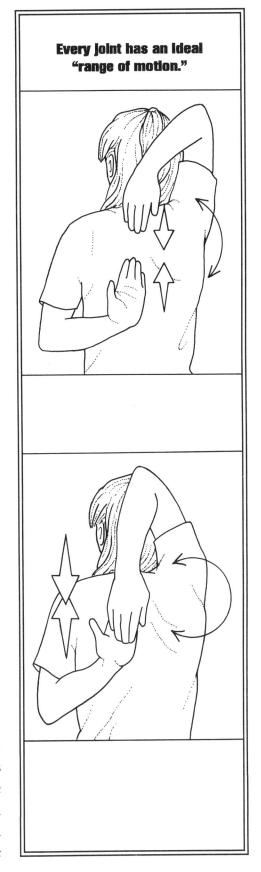

Every joint has an ideal "range of motion."

living a very active physical life, I have never had a serious injury, and I know that is partly because all my life my muscles have been strong.

The strength of a muscle is the ability to exert force over a short period of time. Muscle endurance is the muscle's ability to do something over and over again without tiring out. Both muscle strength and muscle endurance are important to your health. They are also important for playing sports and for doing many things in everyday life. Many sports require good muscle endurance, and some sports—like weightlifting, the field events (such as shotputting and discus), football, rowing, and gymnastics—require considerable strength as well. Muscular strength and the ability of muscles to work for long periods of time without tiring out are not only useful to athletes, but to carpenters, dancers, furniture movers, woodsmen, construction workers, commercial fishermen—all kinds of people who work and play with their bodies.

Muscles are made strong, and build endurance, by working or exercising them *against* something. This kind of exercise is known as resistance exercise. When you do a push-up, your chest, shoulder, and arm muscles are working against the resistance of your own body. Weightlifters and bodybuilders work their muscles against the resistance of the barbells and dumbbells they lift. In the next chapter, I'll tell you how to exercise your muscles against the resistance of your own body in order to make them strong and develop endurance, and at the end of the book, I'll show you some good muscle-strengthening exercises to put into your exercise program.

fat versus lean

Our bodies are composed of "fat weight," which is made up of fatty tissue, and "lean weight," which is made up of the body's internal organs, bone, and muscle tissue. To be physically fit for good health, you shouldn't have too high a percentage of fat weight. According to Dr. Kenneth Cooper, in boys between five and eighteen, the optimal range of body-fat percentage is between 10 percent and

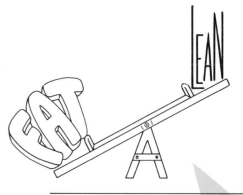

20 percent. In girls of the same age, the optimal range is between 15 percent and 25 percent. A body-fat percentage that is too high is known as obesity, and obesity has been associated by doctors with high blood pressure, heart disease, and many other health problems.

It is a lot of extra work for the body to carry fat around because, unlike muscle, fat doesn't pull its own weight. Bodies that have to lug around a lot of useless fat are not as healthy as lean bodies. They usually can't perform as well at sports, and they have to work harder at all the physical movements of day-to-day living.

If you want to find out how fat you are, a bathroom scale can't really tell you. Because muscle and bone are heavier than fat, it is possible for you to be heavy on the scale and yet lean, or to be light on the scale and yet too fat. The best and healthiest way to control your body fat percentage is through a combination of sensible eating and exercise. Fat is produced when the body is taking in and holding on to more calories than it needs. Sensible, healthful eating can control the number of calories you are taking in, and exercise can help burn off whatever calories you don't need. If you eat smart and get plenty of exercise, you'll never have to worry about being too fat.

To recap, heart-lung strength, joint-muscle flexibility, muscular strength and endurance, and body composition are the four parts of physical fitness for good health. You can see the one thing they all have in common is exercise. In fact, regular exercise and sensible eating are the two keys to health-related physical fitness—both for adults and for kids.

fitness for physical skills

As I said before, you can be physically fit for many different things. Do you remember the example of the kid who could hit a baseball a long way but who couldn't run around the bases without huffing and puffing? Well, that would be a kid who was "physically fit" for the skill of hitting a baseball (which is a hard thing to do), but who had poor "aerobic," or heart/lung, fitness.

As we've already seen, the most important kind of physical fitness is that directly related to good health, but there is another kind of fitness that is almost as important: *fitness for the performance of physical skills.*

Physical, or "motor," skills are the building blocks of bodily movement. Every coordinated movement that we make with our bodies is based on a motor skill, or a number of motor skills put together. We begin acquiring motor skills from the moment we are born, and those early skills —such as grasping, reaching, sucking—become the first building blocks for all our future movements.

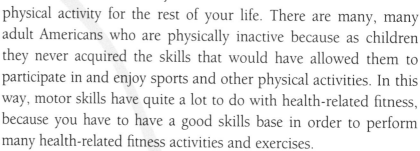

Practically all of the physical skills we ever have are acquired in childhood and early adolescence. Therefore, the more skills we develop before the age of fifteen or sixteen, and the more we perfect those skills, the better we will be at sports and other physical activities when we are older.

Why are motor skills so important? Simply because they form the foundation of all your

physical activity for the rest of your life. There are many, many adult Americans who are physically inactive because as children they never acquired the skills that would have allowed them to participate in and enjoy sports and other physical activities. In this way, motor skills have quite a lot to do with health-related fitness, because you have to have a good skills base in order to perform many health-related fitness activities and exercises.

If a good skills foundation is important to the performance of health-related fitness activities and exercise, it is absolutely crucial to the performance and enjoyment of sports. No one enjoys doing things they cannot do well, and that is particularly true of sports. If you start playing baseball with some of your friends and find out you can't bat or catch or throw well, the chances are good you won't play baseball for very long, and you will probably never come back to it later on in your life. If you begin playing baseball, with good throwing, catching, and batting skills, however, you will perform better at the sport, enjoy it more, and very likely stay with it.

The development of physical skills has considerable importance in areas other than sports and fitness. Good motor skills are neces-

sary in activities as various as flying an airplane, ballet dancing, sculpting, typing, and surgery. With well-developed physical skills, you can go through life able to do things, athletic and otherwise, that require coordination and grace. You, can enjoy your body and take pleasure in the wonderful variety of movements it is capable of.

In Chapter 2, I will tell you more about motor skills and how to develop them, and in Appendix D, you'll find some excellent "skill drills" that you can use to help improve your physical skills for fitness, sports, and everyday life.

fitness for fun

For me the things most fun in life are physical things—skiing, lifting weights, tennis, hiking. I love to do all those activities and lots of others as well, and so do my family and friends. Those are the things we have fun doing, so we keep ourselves fit to do them—fit while having fun.

Fitness isn't like taking medicine—it's simply living in a way that enables you to develop a body strong, flexible, and healthy enough to do all the things in life you want to do with it.

As I told you at the beginning of this chapter, when I was growing up in Austria, my friends and I exercised all the time without even knowing it was exercise. We walked or rode our bikes to and from school; we played soccer and other games outside with our parents every afternoon; and on weekends we went skiing, or hiking, or mountain climbing, or swimming in the lake. We didn't think of ourselves as being physically fit, but we were. We were just living and enjoying a life of good food and plenty of exercise that made us, and kept us, able to do all the fun things we wanted to do.

And that's what I want for you—the fun and good health of a physically active life. I want exercise to become as normal and enjoyable and necessary in your life as it was and still is in mine.

So let's go on now to the next chapter and see how to do that.

Programs

2 putting together your fitness program

The last chapter outlined what physical fitness means for young people your age. As we have seen, what is most important is that you become physically fit for a lifetime of good health with the right kind of exercise and sensible nutrition. It is also important that you continue to build a good, broad base of physical skills that will give you access for the rest of your life to enjoyable participation in sports and fitness activities, and to the pleasures of efficient, graceful physical movement.

Now let's look at how to put those principles into practice by creating a fitness program that combines health-related and skill-related exercises.

In order for a fitness program to work for you, you have to make exercise a normal, necessary, and regular part of your everyday life. Exercising once in a while, though better than never exercising, will not make you or keep you fit. In order to make it easy for you to follow a fitness program *regularly,* and enjoy following it, I have made it possible for you to create that program yourself, especially *for* yourself. You can custom-tailor it, in other words, to fit your own goals and to make it as comfortable as possible for you to use. Or, to use another metaphor, creating your exercise program from this book is a little like eating in a cafeteria. In a cafeteria you can get a tray and go down the line and pick exactly which foods you want to eat. You might get a salad, and I might get a sandwich; you might get chicken, and I might get soup. Both of us can pick whatever we like to eat, and we can change what we get every day so we don't get bored, always eating the same thing. Well, that's the way I've designed these programs—so that you can choose your own exercises, and vary them whenever you like.

Your weekly program will look like this:

my fitness program

▶ **Three Days Per Week:** Five minutes of warm-up;
twenty-five minutes of continuous aerobic exercise;
five minutes of cool-down.

▶ **Two Days Per Week:** Ten minutes of stretching;
twenty-five minutes of strength training;
five minutes of cool-down.

▶ **One Day Per Week:** Five minutes of warm-up;
twenty-five minutes of skill drills;
five minutes of cool-down.

To put this program together for yourself, here is what to do.

In Appendix A of this book is a collection of aerobic exercises. *After* you have read the paragraphs below headed Aerobic Exercise—which will tell you what you need to know about the role aerobic exercise should play in your program, how to do those exercises, and how to warm up for them and cool down afterward—then go to the back of the book and choose the exercise you want to plug into your program (for twenty-five minutes a day, three days a

week). You can use any of the exercises listed in Appendix A, and you can alternate each of them from week to week, or day to day, or even combine two or more of them within the same workout as long as you don't stop between them (for example, you could run for fifteen minutes and bike for ten, for one twenty-five-minute workout). Do the same thing for your stretching and strength training: after you read the sections below headed Flexibility Exercise and Muscular Strength and Endurance Exercise, go to these sections in Appendixes B and C and choose exercises for your fitness program.

In Appendix B, you will find a list of stretching exercises for different parts of your body. The first ones listed for each body part are easy exercises, and the later ones get progressively more advanced. You will probably want to start with an easy stretch or two for each body part (for fifteen minutes, two days a week) when you begin your program, and then work up to the more advanced stretches. As you move ahead with your program, you might want to continue combining stretches for different parts of your body in each flexibility workout, or you might decide to do stretches for just one part of your body for a particular workout.

In Appendix C, you'll find a list of strength exercises for different parts of the body. As with the stretches, the first ones listed for each body part are easy, and the later ones are more advanced. If you have not done any strength training, I recommend you begin the strength segment of your workout (fifteen minutes a day, two days a week) by choosing one or two easy exercises for each body part. You can move on to more advanced exercises as you get stronger; and though you may want to focus on a particular body part occasionally in your workouts (if you're trying to get your legs stronger for soccer, for example; or you want to lose some flab around your waist), I recommend you continue to do some strength exercises for each body part.

Finally, after you have read the section below called Skill Development Exercise, look at Appendix D for a list of exercises to plug into the skills development segment of your workout (one day a week for twenty-five minutes). Pick one or more of those exercises to do for each skills workout.

Here are some more suggestions on how to put your program together and get the most out of it.

▶ It doesn't really matter which days of the week you choose to do your workouts, but I recommend that you alternate your aerobic days with your strength and flexibility days. Your skills workout could come on an aerobic day, on a strength and flexibility day, or on a day by itself. You might want to set up a schedule like this:

▶ **Monday, Wednesday, Friday: Aerobics, 4–4:35 P.M.**

▶ **Tuesday, Thursday: Strength and Flexibility, 5–5:35 P.M.**

▶ **Sunday: Skills, 9–9:35 A.M.**

Or, like this:

▶ **Tuesday, Thursday, Saturday: Aerobics, 4:30–5:05 P.M.**

▶ **Monday, Wednesday: Strength and Flexibility, 4:30–5:05 P.M.**

▶ **Saturday: Skills, 10–10:35 A.M.**

The important thing is to set up a schedule you can follow week in and week out. (Remember to warm up/stretch and cool down/stretch for five minutes before and after each activity.)

▶ Though it is all right to plug different exercises into your program every day if you want to, I suggest that you stick with a particular aerobic exercise and skill drill (or drills) for at least one week at a time. Often it takes that long to get familiar enough with the exercise or drill to get the full fitness benefit from it.

▶ Be sure to read the sections in this chapter that tell you *how* to do the exercises, and then *follow* those instructions. If there is something in the instructions you don't understand, ask one of your parents or a physical education teacher or coach to make it clear to you.

▶ Regularity is the key to any exercise program. Set days, and times during the day, for your workouts when it will be convenient for you to do them. And once you start your program, *stick with it and try not to miss even one workout.* It might take a while before you see or feel any results, but they will come—*if* you stay with it on a regular basis.

▶ Avoid exercising right after you eat, or in the middle of the day in very hot weather, and *always* drink plenty of liquids (water is best) before, during, and after your workouts.

▶ Don't let school or community sports or exercise programs substitute for your fitness program. Many sports programs offer little fitness benefit, and besides, schools and community sports and exercise programs come and go. The point is to make exercise *a daily practice* in your life, and only you can do that for yourself.

▶ It's fun to work out with one or more partners, and a partner can help keep you motivated. Try to get one or both of your parents and/or a friend or two to join you in your workouts. But if nobody wants to join you, do your workouts by yourself; after a while, when people start to notice how strong and fit you are, they'll probably change their minds.

▶ Arrange good places to do your workouts, both outdoors and indoors (for rainy or wintry days). If you don't have a backyard, parks and playgrounds make good outdoor workout places. For indoor workouts, all you need is a room that's well ventilated and big enough and always available to you.

▶ Start your program slowly. Don't overdo it and don't push yourself at first. Injury and/or discouragement can come from trying to do too much too soon, and if you make your program so hard that it's unpleasant, you will very likely quit doing it and become another fitness dropout. So, start with a program that is easy and fun for you to do, and gradually make it harder.

▶ It is good to set goals for yourself, but at first, make them goals that are easy to achieve. If you can do only three push-ups when you first start your program, and you want to get to twenty, set six as your first goal. When you can do six push-ups, set another goal of ten, then of fifteen; and when you can do fifteen, *then* aim for twenty.

▶ You should get your parents to take you for a checkup with your doctor before beginning this or any other exercise program, particularly if you are overweight or have any medical problems.

Now, before you grab a tray and head down the cafeteria line to put your fitness program together, please read the sections below that describe the various types of exercise you'll be doing and tell you how to do them safely and productively.

aerobic exercise

Aerobic exercise is good for you in so many ways that it is almost like a *magic tonic*. It not only strengthens your heart and lungs, it also helps burn off fat, gives you more energy, improves your muscle tone, and even helps you to concentrate and think better. It is the single most important form of exercise you can do, all your life, so use your program as a means to turn it into a lifetime practice.

As you have learned in Chapter 1, aerobic exercise is exercise that makes your heart and lungs deliver more oxygen to your body than usual for an extended period of time. For someone running a marathon, that period of time is usually over two hours; for a tri-athlete, it can be for as long as *eight hours*. For you, we are going to start with twenty-five minutes.

For an aerobic exercise session to really do you any good, continuous movement (exercise) has to be kept up for at least twenty minutes at a brisk level, causing your heart and lungs to work harder than usual, but not too hard.

▶ How do you know when your heart and lungs are working hard enough, but not too hard? There are two ways to tell. The easiest way is to use what I call the "talk test." During your aerobic workouts you should be exercising hard enough so that you are breathing heavily but not so heavily that you can't talk. You should be able to talk to another person or to yourself (with maybe just a little puffing, but not much) *while* you exercise. If you can't, you are exercising too hard. After a few aerobic workouts, you'll learn to "listen to your body." If it tells you, "This isn't hard enough; I'm not even breathing fast," then step up the exercise a little. If it tells you, "Hey, I'm running out of breath here . . . can't talk . . . I'm too hot!"—then slow down. Pretty soon you'll know just how hard you should be exercising.

▶ Another, more scientific and more exact way of knowing whether you're exercising hard enough aerobically is by taking your pulse. Your pulse tells you how fast your heart is beating, or how hard it is working. The level at which your heart has to work for at least twenty minutes for you to get aerobic (health) benefit from that work is called your "target heart rate." According to experts, the target heart rate for kids your age is between 140 and 180 beats per minute. When you are exercising, if your heart is beating more than 180 beats per minute, you are exercising *too* hard and you should slow down a little; if your heart is beating less than 140 beats per minute, you're not exercising hard enough and you should go a little faster. For your aerobic workouts your goal is to get your heart beating at a rate between 140 and 180 beats per minute and to keep it there. The talk test can tell you pretty accurately when you are in that range (if you can't talk, your heart may be beating faster than 180 beats per minute; if you are not breathing heavily, it is probably working at less than 140 beats per minute). But if you want to know exactly how hard your heart is working, you can find out by taking your own pulse while you're exercising and/or immediately after you stop. This is not always easy to do, but if you want to try it, get a coach or a nurse to show you how to take your pulse (it's best taken on the carotid artery in your throat). You should measure your pulse a couple of times during your aerobic exercise and then again *immediately after you stop*. Measure it by counting the number of beats in ten seconds, then multiply that number by six—that will give you your heart rate per minute. You can stop exercising very briefly to take your pulse, but start again immediately after taking it.

▶ For some important tips on how to perform the various aerobic activities, see Appendix A at the back of this book.

flexibility exercise

As small children we are all naturally flexible, but as we enter the puberty years we begin losing joint and muscle flexibility unless we do regular stretching exercises. Good flexibility in joints and muscles helps prevent injuries such as muscle pulls and bad backs; it also is very important to sports performance and helps us move through life more easily and gracefully.

Very few people, adults or children, enjoy stretching exercises when they first begin doing them, and often those exercises can seem like a waste of time. But if you stick with them, you'll find that they *do* become enjoyable, even addictive, and the loose, warmed-up, relaxed feeling they give your body more than justifies the time it takes to do them.

There are two types of stretches—muscle stretches, for muscle flexibility; and range-of-motion stretches, for joint flexibility. It is important to do both. Range-of-motion stretches carry a joint through part or all of its entire range of motion—like swinging (rotating) your arms slowly in a 360-degree circle to exercise the range of motion in your shoulders, or rolling your head around to exercise your neck. A muscle stretch simply stretches a particular muscle out and holds it there for a few seconds.

Any time is a good time to stretch (I do stretches while I'm flying in an airplane, while I'm watching TV or a movie, and while I'm working in my office), but it is particularly good to stretch before and after doing vigorous exercise—before, in order to warm up the muscles, and after, to keep them from getting stiff. I recommend that you do a few stretches before and after your aerobic workouts, in addition to the ten minutes of stretching twice a week before and after your strength workouts.

For some important tips on how to do your stretching exercises, see Appendix B.

muscular strength and endurance exercise

Over 75 percent of America's girls and almost 30 percent of our boys cannot do a single pull-up! This fact indicates that American boys and girls have much less muscular strength and endurance than they need to be physically fit for good health. I'm *not* saying you need big muscles like mine to be healthy, but strong muscles with good endurance improve our posture, protect us from injury, and help keep us from developing lower-back (and other joint and muscle) problems. Muscle strength and endurance are also very important to many sports, particularly ones like tennis and swimming, where certain muscle groups have to keep working over a long period of time. And finally, the kind of exercise that builds muscular strength and endurance (resistance exercise) also keeps our bodies toned up—which means they feel and look better.

Some people think that strength is a boy thing only, but *it is as important to the good health of girls as it is to boys*. Recent studies have shown that improving strength can help avoid osteoporosis among women later in life. Girls between eleven and fifteen years old should do the same strength and muscle endurance exercises given in the back of this book as the boys do, and for all the same reasons.

For a number of reasons, I don't believe that boys and girls under sixteen should train with

weights. The strength and muscular endurance exercises I've included in this book mostly use your body's own weight for resistance (and occasionally books or other light objects) rather than weights, but if you do them as I recommend, you can get the same kind of benefit from them as you can from exercises with weights. These exercises are *not* designed to build big muscles or extreme strength, but rather to develop healthy, usable strength and supple, injury-resistant muscles.

For some guidelines on how to do your strength training, see Appendix C.

skill development exercise

The more physical skills we have and the better developed they are, the better we can do all the physical things we do in life, including sports and fitness activities. By the time you are eleven years old, you already have most of the physical skills you will ever have. However, many of those skills can still be improved, and the more you improve them now, the more likely you are to continue to enjoy exercise, sports, and other physical activities as you get older, and therefore, the more likely you are to stay fit.

The "skill drills" I have included in Appendix D are designed to improve many of the skills that are central to numerous sports and lifetime fitness activities. Among those skills are: whole-body coordination, balance, balance stabilization, foot speed, visual tracking, and agility.

For some important tips on skill drills, see Appendix D.

sample programs

To help you put together your program, here are two sample programs. Program A would be a good beginning program for an eleven- or twelve-year-old who does not exercise much. Program B would be appropriate for a thirteen- or fourteen-year-old who is in pretty good shape. To come up with exactly the right program for you—one that is neither too hard nor too easy and one that you can enjoy doing—you may have to experiment a bit with the exercises. But these sample programs should help get you started.

program a

aerobics

▶ **Monday, Wednesday, Friday (4:30–5:05 P.M.):**
five minutes of warm-up;
twenty-five minutes of alternating jogging and brisk walking;
five minutes of cool-down.

flexibility and strength and muscular endurance

▶ **Tuesday, Saturday (Tuesday, 4:30–5:30 P.M.; Saturday, 9–9:35 A.M.):**
flexibility exercises numbers 1, 5, 7, 9, 10, 14, and 19 (ten minutes);
strength exercises numbers 1, 9, 18, 25, 27, 30, and 31 (twenty minutes).

skills

▶ **Sunday (2–2:35 P.M.):**
five minutes of warm-up;
twenty-five minutes of Agility Run and Blind Stork;
five minutes of cool-down.

program b

aerobics

▶ **Tuesday, Thursday, Saturday (Tuesday and Thursday, 4–4:35 P.M.; Saturday 10–10:35 A.M.):**
five minutes of warm-up;
twenty-five minutes of swimming laps;
five minutes of cool-down.

flexibility and strength and muscular endurance

▶ **Sunday, Wednesday (Sunday, 10–10:35 A.M.; Wednesday, 4–4:35 P.M.):**
flexibility exercises numbers 2, 4, 6, 11, 13, 15, 16, and 17 (ten minutes);
strength exercises numbers 2, 5, 10, 11, 13, 20, 26, 28, 29, and 32 (twenty minutes).

skills

▶ **Sunday (3–3:35 P.M.):**
five minutes of warm-up;
twenty-five minutes of Hexagonal Jump;
five minutes of cool-down.

king on the mountain

I grew up in a small Austrian village called Thal. Thal was a farming community and almost everyone in the village, except for our family, lived on farms. The countryside around the village was quite picturesque —pastures, meadows, and rolling hills where cows and horses grazed on sweet grass, fields of wheat and hay, and many orchards that grew cherries, apples, and pears. My father, Gustav, my mother, Aurelia, and my brother, Meinhard, and I lived in a small house that was surrounded by farms. My father was a big, strong man who excelled at many sports, and he instilled in Meinhard and me a wonderful ethic—to work hard when we were working and to play hard when we were playing.

There was always plenty of physical work around our house. From the time we were very young, Meinhard and I had numerous chores—splitting and stacking wood, carrying coal for the stove, cleaning the stove and oven of ash, and carrying water to the house from our well. But we also managed to find time for play and sports. Both Meinhard and I participated in gymnastics, soccer, and running and jumping events in school. Our lives outside of school were just as active. We had neighborhood championships in badminton and volleyball, sledding on the hills in the winter, and swimming in the lake near our house and hiking in the mountains in the summer. Meinhard and I would devote our time to soccer practice, and my father would leave work early to coach and sometimes play with us. Whenever our village soccer team played other village teams, my father was often asked to referee the game because he was a policeman and considered to be a man of honesty and integrity.

When I was ten years old, I left the two-room schoolhouse in Thal, where my friends and I had gone to school, and started taking the bus every day to a junior high school five miles away in the much bigger town of Graz. In order to get our chores done before the school bus came, Meinhard and I had to get up at 6:00 A.M. After dressing and washing, we would go get fresh milk for my mother from our neighbors the Volroyds (who had a cow), bring in water and wood, and in winter, shovel snow from the paths to the well and the road. After all this work, we'd be ready for a hearty breakfast that usually included hot chocolate and porridge, which my mother made from cornmeal and is called polenta. While Meinhard and I ate breakfast, my mother would pack a lunch for us to take to school. She always included raw carrots and celery, a piece of fruit, and small, homemade loaves of bread that had delicious fruit fillings.

I was lucky in that my two best friends, Sigmund Volroyd and Annaliese Braun, who lived on surrounding farms, were entering junior high with me. But the first few weeks at the new school in Graz were hard for me and my friends from Thal. Since Meinhard was a year older than I was, he had already been at the school for a year, so that made it a little easier. Meinhard would stick up for me and my friends when the kids from the "big city" called us hicks, and he even got into some fights on our account. The truth is we *were* sort of hickish compared to the kids who had grown up in Graz and who had televisions and telephones and things like that in their houses. But if anyone told us that, they'd have a fight on their hands, whether Meinhard was around or not. Annaliese was a girl, but she was as tough and strong as most boys, and none of the three of us was afraid to take on anybody.

Anybody but Franz Steeger, that is. Franz was thirteen and the best athlete in Graz. He was the best runner, jumper, soccer player, and swimmer that anyone could remember ever coming from the town. Franz was also very strong, and he was already beginning to train in the shotput so he could try out for the Austrian team when he got older. At our school, we did a lot of running, rope climbing, wall climbing with pegs, and gymnastic exercises with the "horse," a medicine ball, and the flying rings. Franz was always the best at all those things, and could even do some of them better than the gym teachers.

But Franz was also a bully. He didn't bother me or my friends because we were too young for him to notice us, but he terrorized some of the other kids at the school, even making a few of them carry his books and shine his shoes. Everyone I knew was afraid of Franz, partly because of a rumor that he had once broken the jaw of a grown man, a truck driver who had dented his mother's car.

One day after school, Sig, Annaliese, and I decided to ride our bikes out to the abandoned quarry near Graz. My brother, Meinhard, also joined us. This quarry was where they had blasted and dug out rock to build roads, and big piles of rock and sand had been left that we liked to climb and play on. One of our favorite games was "King on the Mountain," where everyone would scramble for

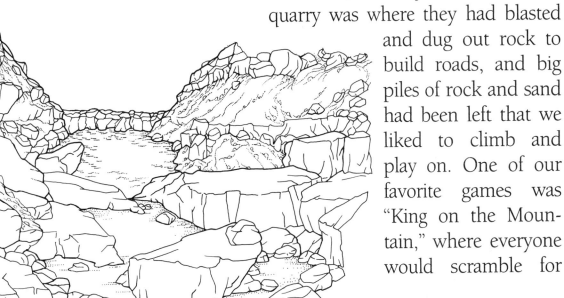

the top of the tallest sandpile and try to keep the others from reaching it. When one person finally got to the top, he tried to keep it for as long as he could by shoving off anyone who tried to take it from him.

It was usually just kids my age who played out at the quarry, but on this particular day, there also was a crowd of seventh- and eighth-graders. And on top of the tallest sandpile stood Franz Steeger. It was the first time I'd ever seen him with his shirt off, and I couldn't believe the muscles in his upper body. He looked like one of the statues of Roman gods I'd seen in our history books.

Heine Kohler, who was in Meinhard's grade, walked over to us. He was all full of sand and breathing hard. He had a bloody nose and he was obviously angry.

"Franz is slugging people. Karl and I almost had him off the top, but he hit me in the nose and he kicked Karl in the knee."

Just then I saw Franz notice us, and he shouted from the top of the sandpile, "Hey, Meinhard—don't waste your time talking to that crybaby. Come see if *you* can take the mountain. The rest of these guys here are weaker than girls."

"Jerk!" shouted Annaliese. I looked over at her, and her eyes were like little bombs as she stared at Franz.

Franz threw back his head and laughed. "You ride around on your bike with girls and little children? I thought you were tough, Meinhard!"

"Well," said Meinhard quietly, "I guess I'll give it a try." He kicked out the stand on his bike and walked toward the sandpile.

"Be careful, Duke," said Siggy. Siggy always called Meinhard "Duke."

"Don't let him hit you in the nose, Meinhard," warned Heine. "It feels like a cow kicked you!"

Meinhard was very wiry and strong, even though he was thin. But looking at Franz, I didn't see how Meinhard could possibly move him off the top of the "mountain." Though I wanted Meinhard to win the contest, I couldn't help admiring the body that Franz had developed and respecting the training work that had gone into it. If you could use that kind of body to bully people, I thought, you could also use it to help and protect

people. And it was at that exact moment that I made up my mind that I, too, would make myself strong. I would work hard to develop a body like Franz's, but I would use it differently.

Meinhard ran up the sandpile and tried to grab Franz by the shoulders, but Franz dodged him and shoved him down the other side of the pile. Meinhard then made a second and a third charge, and both times Franz easily threw him off the mountain. But on his fourth try, Meinhard dove in low and tackled Franz around the knees. Franz fell backward and Meinhard gave his rear end a mighty shove and pushed Franz off the top of the sandpile. He rolled about halfway down it. Annaliese, Sig, Heine, and I started cheering, and most of the older kids standing around below joined us. That must have made Franz mad, because he charged back up the hill with his fists clenched and ready to fly.

"Look out, Meinhard!" shouted Heine.

I could see Meinhard watching Franz come. He raised his own fists. I felt like I had to do something to keep Meinhard from getting hurt.

"Franz!" I shouted in as deep a voice as I could muster.

Franz stopped and looked down to see who was calling him.

"In 'King on the Mountain' it is against the rules to kick or use your fists. You are the best athlete and sportsman that any of us has ever known, and we are sure that you would not ever want to break the rules of a game."

Franz stared at me for what seemed like forever.

"If he comes down here for Arnold, you and I will jump on his back, Siggy," Annaliese whispered fiercely.

But Franz didn't come. He just stared at me for a long time, as if he was thinking, and then he grinned. "You are right," he said. Then he walked up the sandpile and shook hands with Meinhard.

"Well done," I told Franz under my breath, and I knew that one day, he and I could be friends.

It is rare that we learn two lessons at once from anyone. But Franz the bully taught me two important things that day, two lessons I have treasured all my life: that training and hard work really do pay off; and that no one is entirely what he or she *seems* to be.

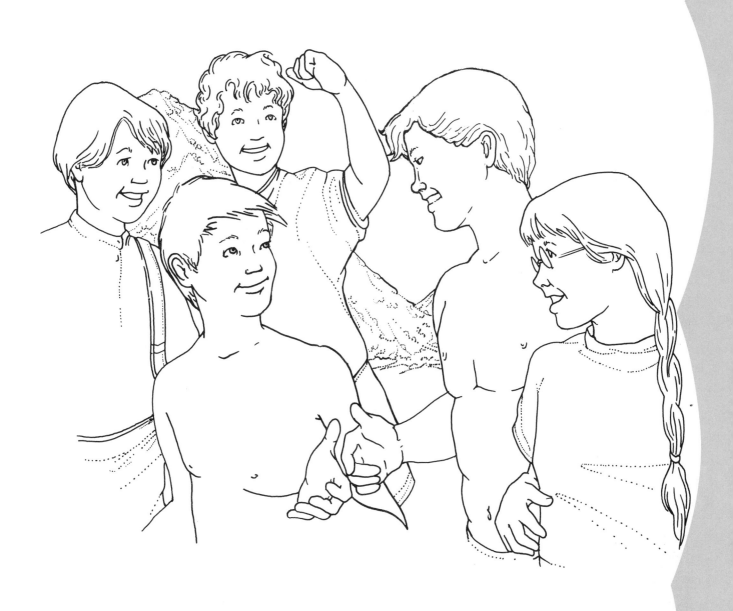

NUTRITION

3 eating smart

Regular exercise is one half of the foundation of
lifetime fitness and good health. The other half
is good nutrition, or what I call "eating smart."
You've probably heard the old saying
"You are what you eat." Well, it's
true: if you get good, nutritious,
healthful food, you feel well,
look well, and perform well.
If all you eat for snacks are
cookies and cupcakes,

you'll begin to look like a Twinkie, and your muscles will feel soft and "creamy" instead of like strong muscle tissue.

A comparison I like to use is one in which your body is like a car and what you eat is like the fuel that goes into that car. A good balanced diet of nutritious foods is high-test fuel, and your body and mind are able to run well on it without breakdowns. A bad diet is watered-down fuel that your body cannot run well on; and if the diet is bad enough, it is comparable to putting sugar into your gas tank, which means that sooner or later, you will have to go in for repair of your fuel lines (heart, arteries, and veins).

I'm not kidding about that. Of the ten leading causes of death in America, five—athero-sclerosis, stroke, heart disease, diabetes, and cancer—can be caused by bad diet. High blood pressure, obesity, and osteoporosis can also be caused by what and how much you eat. Eating dumb, in short, can make us sick, and even kill us. It also robs us of energy, makes our bodies soft and fat, and keeps us from performing well at sports, at school, and on the job.

In this chapter, I'll tell you how to eat smart—for good health, good looks, and good performance—and I'll give you some smart eating and cooking tips for you to pass along to your parents, so that your whole family can enjoy the many benefits of good nutrition.

First of all, you should understand that eating smart does *not* mean all sprouts and tofu. Good eating can and should be delicious eating, and once you get used to it, you'll feel sorry for those poor slobs at the take-out window of fast-food places. Good nutrition is not about fads either. Where I grew up no one had ever heard of grapefruit diets or vitamin supplements or fish oil—we just ate good, home-cooked country food and grew up healthy and strong on it, the same way our parents and grandparents had.

Eating smart is knowing what is good for you and what is not. Then it is the simple discipline of practicing that knowledge in the form of good eating habits until those habits become second nature. You'll find it is just as easy, or easier, to make a habit of eating smart as it is to make a habit of eating junk food.

Let's look at a few of the things that are good for you and a few of the things that are not:

the "bad dudes"

fats: Fat is a good source of energy and provides the body with a number of important nutrients, but most Americans have diets that are much too high in fats, particularly in what are called saturated fats, which come mostly from meats and dairy products such as cheese, cream, and whole milk. The saturated fats that we get too much of every day—from fast food, lunch meats, red meats, butter, cream, and desserts—are known to cause a variety of health problems, including heart disease and cancer.

cholesterol: Cholesterol is another "bad" fat that comes mostly from meats and dairy products and that Americans eat too much of (over 30 percent of American kids twelve to fifteen years old have abnormally high cholesterol levels). Unsaturated fats that come from olives, nuts, seeds, and vegetables (such as corn oil, olive oil, walnut oil, canola oil) are much better for you than saturated fats. One good way to cut down on the "bad fat" in your diet is to use only polyunsaturated fats to cook with and in your salad dressings.

salt: Americans eat too much salt, and too much salt in your diet can lead to high blood pressure and strokes, and can cause premenstrual water retention and bloating in women. Fast foods and snack foods such as potato chips, crackers, and popcorn are often loaded with salt, as are many canned, packaged, and frozen foods. You should be conscious of how much salt is in the foods you eat (check the can or box for sodium content), and use it only sparingly or not at all as a spice on foods.

One twelve-ounce cola contains nine teaspoons of sugar.

One fast-food hamburger with cheese contains nine teaspoons of solid fat.

sugar: Too much sugar in your diet can cause, or contribute to, diabetes, obesity, some forms of cancer and heart disease, hypoglycemia, dental cavities, and bowel and stomach problems. You would think then that people would be careful how much sugar they eat, but the great majority aren't. In fact, the typical American eats five or six times more sugar than he or she needs; 99 percent of American kids eat sweet desserts at least six times a week; and, on average, American kids drink twenty-four ounces of soda pop (which is full of sugar) a day. That is certainly not being careful about how much sugar we eat! You can cut down on your sugar consumption by eating less candy, ice cream, cookies, pies, and cakes and other sweet foods, and by drinking only diet soft drinks—if you have to drink soft drinks at all (fruit juices taste better and are better for you). As with salt, many foods—such as ketchup, salad dressings, soups, relishes—can carry a "secret" sugar content.

the "good dudes"

proteins: Proteins play a major role in building bone, muscle, blood, skin, and hair, and it is important for adolescents to have plenty of good protein in their diets. We get proteins from vegetables, grains, cereals, dairy products, and meats, but some sources are better for our health than others. The protein we get from red meats and lunch meats comes along with fat, so it is better to get protein from fish and chicken. Other good protein sources are cereals, nuts, low-fat cheese and milk, and beans.

carbohydrates: The complex carbohydrates that we get from vegetables, fruit, pasta, cereals, and grains are the best body fuels around. Foods high in complex carbohydrates are high-energy foods—great for athletes and anyone else who wants to perform well—and are also rich in vitamins, minerals, and often protein. You should make sure your diet is made up of at least 50 percent complex carbohydrates *daily*.

fiber: According to the American Health Foundation, 50 percent of all breast cancers and 75 percent of all colon cancers could be prevented in this country if Americans ate fewer fats *and* increased the amount of fiber in their diets. Fiber also helps prevent rectal cancer, hemorrhoids, and constipation. We get fiber from vegetables, fruits, breads, and bran and whole-grain cereals.

Based on the above list of nutritional good guys and bad guys, these are the things that are wrong with the diet of the average person, young and old, in this country (including, probably, *you*):

▶ We eat too much sugar and salt (much of it coming from fast foods, snacks, and soft drinks).

▶ Our diets are too heavy in cholesterol and saturated fats (from fast foods, again, and lunch meats, snack foods, fatty red meats, butter, cream, and desserts).

▶ We don't eat *enough* of the bran cereals, whole-grain foods, pastas, rice, beans and peas, fresh vegetables and fruits that supply us with nonfat proteins, fiber, and complex carbohydrates.

▶ Our diets are rarely well balanced among the four basic food groups: *protein foods,* such as meat, fish, poultry, eggs, cheese; *dairy products,* such as milk, cheese, and yogurt; *fruits and vegetables;* and *grains and cereals,* including bread, beans and peas, rice, pastas, and potatoes. Also, an unbalanced diet does not provide us with all the vitamins and minerals we need.

You might be thinking, "Okay, Arnold, I've heard all of this before and I *know* I eat like a dummy, but I don't know *how* to eat smart."

Well, it's actually a lot easier than you think, and the best place to start is with:

breakfast

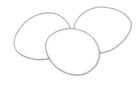

This is, by far, the most important meal of the day, especially for kids your age, and it should *never* be skipped or skimped. Studies have proven that people who eat breakfast are more productive and alert, tend to study better and perform better at sports, than people who do

not. A *good* breakfast provides you with high-test fuel to run on for the whole day; a bad breakfast (a lot of sugar and/or fat) is the same as putting sugar in your gas tank.

Eating smart at breakfast means getting Vitamin C, calcium, potassium, iron, fiber, and complex carbohydrates. A breakfast that would provide all of this is simple: a bowl of unsugared or *lightly* sugared cereal or oatmeal with low-fat milk and some sliced fruit on top; a glass of orange or grapefruit juice; and a piece of whole-grain toast or an English muffin topped with All Fruit preserves. Waffles and whole-grain pancakes topped with fruit instead of syrup are good too, and eggs are fine two to three times a week (unless there is a history of high cholesterol in your family). Make bacon, ham, and sausage once-in-a-while treats, and skip altogether doughnuts, Danish pastries, Pop Tarts, and anything else that is full of sugar.

lunch

Lunch should be a refill, but again, only with high-test fuel. If you have any question about the quality of the lunches at your school (the lunches at many schools are too high in fat, cholesterol, sugar, and salt, and those at many other schools are so tasteless that no one wants to eat them), you should arrange with your parents to help you take your lunch to school from home at least two or three times a week. Good high-test lunch foods are fruit, peanut butter (try to get the nonhydrogenated kind), whole-grain breads, pasta dishes, raw vegetables, nonfat or low-fat yogurt, unsalted nuts, low-sodium soups, and

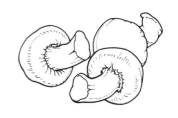

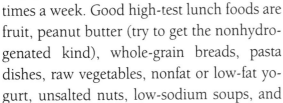

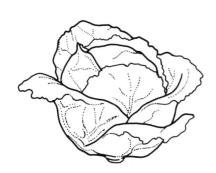

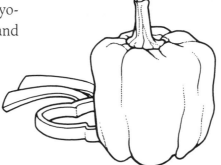

low-fat cheeses. Avoid lunch meats, most of which are way high in fats, and make lunch (or dinner, for that matter) at fast-food restaurants a no-more-than-thrice-a-week treat. (A typical fast-food meal is about 40 percent fat and 20–30 percent sugar, with virtually no fiber and much too much cholesterol and salt—twice or three times a week of that is enough!)

dinner

Try to have your evening meal together with your parents as often as you (and they) can—it gives you not only a chance to share the day with one another but an opportunity to turn smart eating into an enjoyable family ceremony. Everyone should turn off the TV, put away the paper, take the phone off the hook, and sit around the table and *enjoy* a good, well-prepared nutritious meal together. That's what family dinners are all about, and those kinds of meals help remind everyone

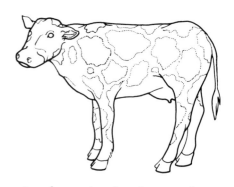

that eating is something to be taken seriously, and to be done with care and style. The more attention you pay to how and what you eat in the home, particularly at dinnertime when you are all together, the more likely it is that you will develop smart eating as a lifetime habit.

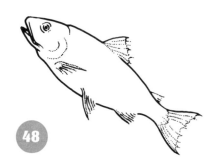

Dinners don't have to be huge—in fact, it's better for you if

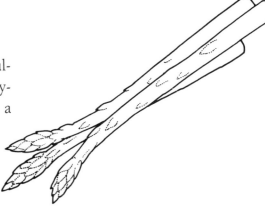

they are not. You should have some good protein (fish, poultry, or lean meat, or beans or peas); some complex carbohydrates (a baked potato, pasta, rice, or steamed vegetables); a little whole-grain bread; and maybe some fruit for dessert.

snacks

There is nothing wrong with snacks, as long as they are the right kind; they can be very helpful as energy pick-me-ups during the day. Candy bars, jelly doughnuts, potato chips, cookies, and cupcakes are *not* the right kind of snacks, and can actually *rob* you of energy. Raw vegetables, fresh fruits, unsalted nuts, nonfat or low-fat yogurt, oatmeal cookies, bran muffins, raisins, cereal, whole-grain breads and crackers, unhydrogenated peanut butter, fruit juice, gorp or trail mix—these are all the *right* kinds of snacks, and you'll find you can very quickly come to prefer them over the wrong kinds.

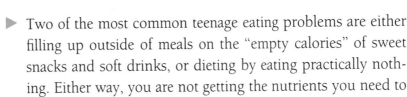

You see how easy smart eating can be? Now here's a list of tips to help you put it into practice in your everyday life.

▶ Two of the most common teenage eating problems are either filling up outside of meals on the "empty calories" of sweet snacks and soft drinks, or dieting by eating practically nothing. Either way, you are not getting the nutrients you need to "run" on. You could also be endangering your health and making it difficult for your body and mind to perform well.

▶ Instead, you should establish for yourself consistent eating patterns, including three well-balanced meals a day of a variety of foods that add up to at least 50 percent carbohydrates, 20 percent protein, and (no more than) 30 percent fat.

▶ Don't eat more than you need—push away from the table *before* you are full.

▶ Eat less sugar and salt, and eat less fat in the form of red meats, butter, cream, etc.

▶ Eat *more* poultry and fish, vegetables and fruits, cereals and grains.

▶ Eat fewer fried foods.

▶ Eat only low-calorie, low-salt, low-sugar, low-fat snacks (if you think that doesn't leave much, you're wrong!).

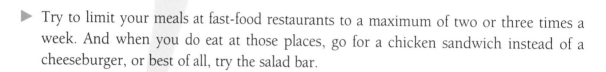

▶ Drink six to eight glasses of liquid, preferably water, every day.

▶ Eat slowly, chew your food well, and only *eat* while you're eating. No TV or reading. Also, try to eat every meal sitting at a table, not while standing, walking around, or driving.

▶ If you have to skip a meal, never let it be breakfast.

▶ Try to limit your meals at fast-food restaurants to a maximum of two or three times a week. And when you do eat at those places, go for a chicken sandwich instead of a cheeseburger, or best of all, try the salad bar.

▶ Young women just beginning to menstruate need lots of iron in their diet. Cereals (particularly iron-enriched), whole-grain breads, eggs, dried fruit, and meats (especially liver) are all good sources of iron. If you think you are not getting enough iron, you might want to take an iron supplement (consult your family doctor about this).

▶ Other than above, you shouldn't need to take vitamins if you eat a balanced diet.

▶ If you are considering a vegetarian diet, first check with your physician, then make sure the diet is a well-balanced one and not just salads. Include in it beans and peas, pastas, rice, fresh vegetables, nuts, cheese, and eggs, as well as plenty of fruit. Some vegetarian diets are low in protein and calcium, so I advise you not to leave out dairy products.

Most of your eating is probably still being done in your home. So I have also prepared a short list of smart eating tips for the family. Maybe your parents are already eating smart, and helping you to do so. If not, pass these tips along to them and recommend that you all follow them—then everyone in your family will benefit from the same good nutritional practices.

▶ Learn how to cook without fats, to make good low-fat, low-salt salad dressings, to steam vegetables, to make your own nutritious whole-grain breads and pastas, and to make desserts without sugar.

▶ Try to eat less butter and cream, and use less salt as a spice and in cooking.

▶ There are lots of excellent healthful-eating cookbooks around—get a couple for the family and use them. You'll find that healthful cooking and eating are *fun*, as well as delicious and good for you.

▶ Get everyone in the family involved in meal planning, shopping, cooking, table setting, and cleaning up. Discuss foods with one another—what's good for you and what's not and why.

▶ To parents: don't keep food in the house that you don't want your kids to eat. *Do* keep plenty of the foods they and you should be eating, and make it easily available all the time, such as fruit in a basket.

▶ Try to acquire tastes for new foods that are healthful and nutritious and also good-tasting, and work them into your menus. Yams, watercress, parsnips, kiwifruit, turnip greens, and pinto beans are just a few examples of nutritious foods that can be prepared deliciously to introduce a little variety into your family meals.

▶ At meals, serve only the amount of food the family needs to eat rather than tempting them with excess food.

▶ And finally, eating, like exercise, is one of the great pleasures of life. Do it smart, but *enjoy it,* and encourage one another to enjoy it.

weight and eating problems

underweight

It is perfectly normal for some boys and girls who are in the "growth spurt" years of puberty to be a little thin, and as their vertical growth slows, most of them fill out. Also, some people, male and female, have a normally thin body type all their lives (a body type known as ectomorphic), and in fact, that is a much healthier way to be than to be overweight. But if you are thinner than you would like to be and want to gain some weight, here are a few tips that might help you put on a few pounds:

▶ Don't snack before meals—it tends to cut your appetite for the foods that can best help you gain weight.

▶ Don't skip meals, and take your time eating them.

▶ Don't try to gain weight by eating more sweet and fatty foods. Instead, eat more whole-grain breads, pastas, potatoes, peanut butter, and bran, fruit, and corn muffins.

▶ *Don't* stop exercising in order to gain. In fact, resistance exercise—particularly a well-supervised weight-training program—is a great way to *help* yourself gain weight.

▶ Try drinking a high-protein drink before you go to bed. (A lot of bodybuilders do this to put on pounds.) One I like is made up of a cup of 2 percent milk, a tablespoon of honey, a banana, and a few spoonfuls of one of the high-protein, weight-gaining formulas available at health food stores.

overweight

Being overweight is a major concern and fear among adolescents, particularly among teenage girls. In fact, many girls believe they are fat when they really aren't. According to a survey of five hundred girls in grades four through twelve conducted by Laurel Mellin, founder of the Shapedown weight-loss program for adolescents, 58 percent of the girls thought they were fat—but only 15 percent were *actually* overweight! The study also showed that close to 80 percent of the ten- and eleven-year-old girls were dieting, and around 70 percent of the twelve- to sixteen-year-olds were trying to lose weight. The fact that dieting is being practiced by that many teenage girls, many of whom don't need it, worries many health experts, and it worries me. Diets can interfere with a number of important growth processes during puberty, and even stunt growth. And if dieting becomes obsessive, it can lead to dangerous, even life-threatening eating disorders and practices.

In terms of our health, it is more dangerous to be *overfat* than overweight. (You might be heavier than others your height and age because you are more muscular.) To determine whether or not you are overfat, get a trained coach, doctor, or physical education teacher to measure your body-fat percentage.

▶ The real secret to losing weight and keeping it off is to eat less and exercise more. And you don't necessarily have to eat less of everything—just of the foods that tend to make people fat, sweets and fatty foods in particular.

▶ Always eat breakfast. A recent study showed that people who ate a hearty breakfast, a reasonably sized lunch, and an early and light dinner (with no evening snacks) lost more weight than did people who ate only dinner or three equal-sized meals. Drink more liquids (water or fruit juice), particularly shortly before eating—it will help fill you up. Exercising just before meals also cuts down on the appetite for many people.

▶ When you feel like snacking, have some fruit or vegetable sticks. And substitute fruit for sweet desserts.

▶ You have a better chance of losing weight and keeping it off if your family exercises and watches calories with you.

▶ Eat slowly, chew slowly, and don't read or watch TV while you eat.

▶ Set *reasonable* weight-loss goals for yourself, and don't try to lose too much too soon.

▶ Continue to eat from all four of the basic food groups.

▶ There are no miracle diets, so don't waste time trying to find one. Weight and fat control is simply a matter of eating the right foods, not overeating, and exercising regularly.

obesity, anorexia nervosa, and bulemia

If you are very overweight, you may be medically obese, which can be a dangerous condition. If you think you might be obese, you should consult your family physician and get started on a medically supervised weight-loss program. Anorexia nervosa and bulemia are psychiatric eating disorders, primarily affecting women and adolescent girls. Anorexia is the chronic practice of eating nothing or very little, even though the individual is hungry, and bulemia is the chronic practice of eating large amounts of food and then throwing it up. Both conditions are dangerous and potentially life-threatening, and should be treated by a doctor.

a final note on alcohol, drugs, and tobacco
DON'T USE THEM, OR I'LL BE BACK!

the rabbit and the rhino

The year I turned thirteen, my junior high school had one of the best soccer teams in eastern Austria. My best friend, Siggy Volroyd, and I were on the team as defensemen. And my other best friend, Annaliese Braun, would have been on the team as well—she was as good a wing as anyone in school. But you see, Annaliese was excluded because she was a girl, and our team was an all-boy team.

That year we finished our season 18 and 0 with one tie, and we won the regional tournament. Annaliese went to every game we played and every practice we had, and sort of acted as our manager and trainer. She was somewhat bossy and tended to think she knew more than anybody else because two of her brothers had been on the Austrian national team. But the fact was, she *did* know a lot, and if a player would listen to her when she told him what he was doing wrong, it would almost always improve his play. When Sig and I had first met her, when we were eight, she had taught us that in soccer it wasn't enough just to be able to kick the ball a long way, but one also had to learn how to dribble well. We had taken her advice, improved our dribbling, and become much better players.

Some of the other boys on our team had started off by laughing at Annaliese whenever she tried to give them a pointer or two. Annaliese was thin and wore glasses, and she had a very serious face, though she also had a wonderful smile whenever she showed it to you. She would walk up to a player, looking very serious like a school teacher, and say something like, "You're not playing deep enough on defense," or, "You need to improve your left footwork," and the guy would just die laughing at first. That is, until he found out that Annaliese was exactly right.

The summer before this particular season, Annaliese had told me that I had gotten too heavy with all the calisthenics I was doing to build my muscles up, and that I would be more valuable to the soccer team if I lost some weight and started running more.

"In a tight game," she said with her serious look, "the team that wins is the one whose defensemen get the least tired."

So Siggy and I ran all summer. We ran everywhere we went. We even ran after supper, up a hill near our house, before we went to bed. By autumn we were thin, and I had lost a lot of the muscle I had put on the winter before, but we could run all day, like wolves, without getting tired. We didn't know the word then, but Sig and I had gotten in great "aerobic" shape and, just as Annaliese had said, it helped us win a lot of tight games over the season.

After our team won the regional tournament, the village of Thal threw a day-long "sports day" and picnic to celebrate. We had these sports days all the time when I was growing up. Farmers would take the day off, housewives would stop their baking and washing, and practically the whole town—kids, babies, old people, everyone—would go out to a huge meadow, a kind of fairground, where we would have games and sports all day long, and a big barbecue picnic in the middle of the day. All morning there would be greasy-pig wrestling, sack races, kite flying, long-jumping and pole-vaulting competitions, shotputting, javelin throws, woodchopping contests, polka dances, and all kinds of other activities.

Then we would feast on barbecued lamb, fresh vegetables and fruits from the rich fields all around us, homemade breads and fruit strudels. After the big meal, we would sit back and relax and enjoy a couple of hours of music. The day would usually end with a pick-up soccer game that was often refereed by my father.

On this particular play day, the game was between our school team and a team made up of all-stars who had already graduated from the school. The captain of that team was Franz Steeger, the best soccer player who had ever gone to our school. I had not seen Franz since he left the school, but I knew he was living in Graz and training for the Austrian shotputting team. When he came out onto the field to warm up, I could feel everyone on our team get a little nervous, myself included. Franz was even more muscular than when we had seen him last—his biceps muscles were big as grapefruits, and his legs were as big as butternut trees.

"Huh!" said Annaliese when she saw him. "Don't worry about Tarzan; he'll never make it through the second half carrying all that weight around. Soccer is a game for rabbits, not rhinos."

My father, who was already out in the field with his whistle around his neck, heard what she said and grinned at me.

But going into the last quarter of the game, it looked as if Annaliese for once might be wrong. Franz had played brilliantly at both ends of the field. He had scored four of his team's five goals (we also had five goals), and he didn't seem to be tiring out at all. But Annaliese wasn't convinced. "He's running out of gas, Arnold," she kept hissing in my ear whenever I came to the sidelines. "Make him *run*—make him chase you. All we need is one goal!"

But we couldn't score that go-ahead goal. At certain times it seemed as if Franz were ten players, all over the field at once—cutting off passes, stealing the ball . . . and then about halfway through the quarter, Pepe, our top scorer all year, twisted his ankle so badly, he couldn't even walk on it. My father, who was coaching both teams as well as refereeing the game, came over to talk to us. He was smiling.

"I'm making this substitution, and I don't want any argument from you boys. Annaliese is going in to play for Pepe."

There were a lot of groans, but nobody would talk back to my father . . . or practically nobody, that is.

"Listen, Herr Schwarzenegger, I don't think—" started Annaliese.

"No argument from any girls, either. Go change, Annaliese. You can wear Pepe's shirt and Rudolf's shoes—he has the smallest feet. Now hurry up, Rabbit—your rhino's waiting."

When we brought the ball back into play, I saw Franz standing at mid-field, his hands on his knees, looking at Annaliese with a wide, devilish grin on his face. But the grin wasn't there for long. Flicking the ball back and forth between her feet as though it were on rubber bands, Annaliese was a one-woman dribbling show. She darted between Franz and his teammates, quick and elusive as a trout, and within minutes Franz really *was* looking tired.

With two minutes to go and the score still tied, one of their wings dribbled into our end and made a long pass to Franz. Earlier in the game, Franz would have gotten to the ball, but now he didn't have the speed left and Sig beat him to it. Sig passed the ball to Annaliese and she dribbled

it up the right sideline. Franz came in on her at an angle and I was afraid
he might make one of the vicious sliding tackles on her that he had been
famous for in school and that had broken a couple of opponents' ankles.
But he only went for the ball. Annaliese faked one way and then passed
to me as I angled in on their goal from mid-field. I had nobody but their
goalie in front of me, but I could hear Franz coming up fast behind. I
thought he would catch me, as I had seen him catch hundreds of would-
be scorers in other games, and I could actually hear the sound of his
huffing breath over my shoulder. I turned on a burst of speed, as my legs
still felt light and strong, and then I no longer heard Franz and I knew I
had him beaten. Their goalie didn't have a chance—I faked low and put
the ball in the upper-left-hand corner of the net.

The next thing I knew, Annaliese had jumped up on my back and was riding me like a horse and Sig was pumping my hand. I was walking over to the sidelines, still carrying Annaliese piggyback, when Franz approached us. His eyes were still fierce with competition, but he was smiling.

"Good goal," he said to me. "I thought I had you, but when you turned up the speed, I couldn't stay with you. And you," he said to Annaliese, "what a dribbler you are—it's like chasing a ghost! You can be on my team anytime, and if any of these boys give you a hard time about playing because you are a girl, you come and see me."

"Thank you," said Annaliese in a whisper. I had never heard her voice that quiet.

SCHOOL

4 physical education and sports participation

Important as they are, school physical education classes and organized sports programs cannot and should not replace your own personal exercise program. Why not? First, because many sports programs and physical education classes do not provide you with enough exercise, and/or the right kind of exercise, to make you and keep you fit. Second, because sports and physical education programs stop and start—no one program is ever on a daily basis throughout the year, and exercise for fitness needs to be done on a *regular* basis. And third, because what you are after is the *lifetime habit of exercise,* and that habit is best developed by creating your own fitness program and continuing to adapt it as you get older. (PE, of course, stops when you get out of school, and many sports—including all the team sports—get harder and harder to arrange to do as you get older.)

But while physical education and sports cannot replace your personal fitness activity, they *can* be extremely valuable supplements to that activity. In this chapter I will provide you, and your parents, with some guidelines on what quality physical education is, and give you some tips on how to get the most out of *your* physical education classes. Then we will take a look at a couple of model PE programs. Finally, I will share a few thoughts with you on sports participation.

In my position as chairman of the President's Council on Physical Fitness and Sports, I have visited a number of middle schools and junior highs all over America and have had a first-hand look at their physical education programs. Some of those programs are excellent; the great majority of them are not. Many parents don't know if the physical education program in their child's school is any good or not, or whether or not the school's lunch program is a healthful, nutritious one. No doubt some parents don't care, but many more simply *assume* that the nutritional and physical activity needs of their kids are being met by the schools. More often than not, those parents are wrong.

I believe that parents owe it to themselves, and to you, to know exactly what your school is doing with respect to physical education, health education, and nutrition. If they find that your school is *not* doing a good job in those areas, they might decide to encourage the school to improve, and often schools *will* improve when pressured to do so by parents. Let's look at how to evaluate how well, or poorly, your school is contributing to your fitness and health. Ideally:

▶ You are "taking" physical education five times a week and your classes are a minimum of thirty minutes long.

▶ There are enough facilities and equipment for every student in every class.

▶ Your teachers are qualified physical education instructors.

▶ PE opportunities are equal for boys and girls, and there are also opportunities for disabled kids, kids with chronic diseases such as asthma, obese kids, and kids who are unskilled at sports.

▶ All kids in your school are tested at least twice a year for the key health-related fitness components, and parents are informed of the results.

▶ Your physical education classes provide each child with at least fifteen minutes of nonstop aerobic exercise three days a week. They also include some stretching and muscular strength and endurance exercise.

▶ You are getting some instruction in the "lifetime fitness activities" (for example, running, walking, swimming, tennis, skiing).

▶ Team sports at your school allow, even encourage, kids who are not good athletes to play.

▶ You are receiving classroom health education on the benefits of exercise; nutrition; drug and alcohol abuse; weight control; and so forth.

▶ Your school has a healthful, nutritious lunch program.

▶ Your school has no junk food vending machines.

If all of the above points are true, you are one of the lucky few in America who is getting from his school quality physical education, supplemental health education, and a good lunch

program. If all of the above points are *not* true, the school is not doing everything it should to meet the fitness needs of its students.

Once you and your parents know that, they may or may not decide to try to do something about it. If they decide to make a few waves and try to improve the system, here is the best way to go about it. Your parents should:

▶ Determine exactly and specifically what it is they want to accomplish. It is much more effective to go to a principal or superintendent with concrete suggestions (for example, "We need more exercise mats"; "We need twice-a-year fitness testing") than with a general complaint.

▶ Get your physical education instructor and the school's PE director, if there is one, on your parents' side at the very beginning. Most physical educators want a good program as much as parents do, and are natural allies in seeking improvement.

▶ Understand the financial situation of your school's physical education department. How much money does it have? How does it get its funding? Can it get more and, if so, how? Most schools whose PE programs are not up to snuff will blame it on a lack of funds. Sometimes that's the real reason, sometimes it's not. If money is not the issue, your parents should find out what the problem really is. And if the lack of money really is the main issue, they should try to come up with some workable and creative solutions to overcome this problem.

▶ Get other parents and the PTA behind them early on—they should speak to anyone else who might share their concerns and put together a lobbying group.

▶ Understand the chain of command in your school and school system and how to negotiate within this system to achieve both your goals and theirs.

After your parents have done all this, they are ready to make a move. If your physical education instructor or teacher would prefer to work within the system for changes, parents should let him try it. But if he doesn't take the initiative, or takes it and fails, your parents should go with a number of other parents to see the school principal and present either a written or verbal petition for change. If your principal can't or won't act, parents should go to see the school district's superintendent. If that doesn't work, they should go to the school board with the parents' committee position. And if *that* doesn't work (it probably will, if they approach the board properly and have the finances figured out), they should tell the whole scroungy lot that they're calling in The Terminator!

what you can do

Here are a few things that *you* can do to get the most out of the physical education program at your school, regardless of how good that program is, and regardless of what—if anything—your parents might try to do to improve the program:

▶ *Participate and enjoy*—don't be a sideline sitter. Come to class every day prepared to participate in, and *enjoy,* the activity planned for that day. Physical education is not busy work, it's not just a way to kill a few minutes in the school day, and it's not punishment. Among other things, it's a great opportunity to learn how to do and enjoy a variety of physical activities, but you have to participate to do that.

▶ *Be willing to take a risk*—for many kids, the single biggest stumbling block to taking full advantage of their PE program is the fear of looking silly or making a mistake— "dropping the ball" in front of peers. To get the maximum benefit from your physical education classes, you *have* to be active and involved, even if doing so means risking a little embarrassment. So dive in, and remember that risk-taking, in all areas of life, is essential to living fully.

▶ *Practice*—at whatever activity you're doing in PE on your own time, after school, or on weekends, with friends and family.

▶ *Communicate*—with your physical education teacher about what's going on in the class, the exercise you do outside of class, any physical limitations you might have, or particular physical talents. If you show interest in what's going on, you might be surprised at how much more interest is shown in return. Like most teachers, your PE instructor probably *loves* what he or she does and appreciates your interest in it.

two model physical education programs

The most common excuse I hear around the country for why a school's physical education program is not as good as it should be (or, in some cases, for why the school doesn't even *offer* PE) is a lack of money. To my mind, that is not an excuse. Good physical education programs do not have to be expensive, as is illustrated by the first model program described below. And if a school *wants* to have a first-rate physical education program, even a very expensive one, ways can be found to pay for it, as is illustrated by the second program described.

I am outlining these two programs here to illustrate to you and your parents what quality physical education is, and also for the sake of any middle school and junior high PE teachers who might be looking for some new ideas to try out in their classrooms. I believe that every child in America has a right to the sort of quality physical education embodied in these two programs.

tom walton's health-related fitness class, rundlett junior high school, concord, new hampshire

At Rundlett Junior High School, Tom Walton has found a way to combine health education and exercise into a single, exceptionally well-integrated and imaginative class, and to do it very inexpensively. His class, an elective, is taught to ninth-graders five days a week for fifty-five minutes, and alternates daily between sports/exercise and classroom health education. One of the reasons the class is so cost effective for the school is that Tom is certified to teach both physical education and health education, so the school is getting one class in place of two without sacrificing quality. Tom, who is a top weightlifter and competitive canoeist, designed the class himself and persuaded the Rundlett principal to let him teach it. It is now one of the school's most popular classes.

On alternating days the kids in Tom's class learn about male and female adolescent health, birth control, pregnancy, body-image issues, sexuality, peer pressure, drugs, alcohol and tobacco, concerns about the need to be beautiful or handsome, and family-crisis counseling. Tom also addresses such issues as dealing with stress, good nutrition, eating disorders, dealing with emotional ups and downs and competitiveness, as well as health-related fitness, avoiding sports injuries, and various forms of exercising. Tom believes that for fitness practices to really "stick" with a kid and be adopted as lifetime habits, they are best introduced in a broad context of health-related education. That learning process takes place every other day in the classroom and then on alternate days some of it is activated by the exercise, or "lab," component of the class.

Tom believes in keeping *every kid in the class* as active as possible for the entire fifty-five minutes on exercise days, so he avoids games and sports in which some kids play and others watch. Instead, he invents and adapts ones in which everybody can participate, get a good workout, and enjoy themselves. In the spring and fall, his class participates in: soccer (with the emphasis on a good aerobic workout rather than the score); ultimate Frisbee (a great aerobic conditioner and lots of fun for a big group); ultimate football (similar to ultimate Frisbee, this is a two-hand-touch, aerobicized version of football); variations of softball; and cross-country running. In the winter, the class does everyone-involved versions of basketball, floor hockey, speedball (a fun, crazy combination of soccer and ultimate Frisbee), indoor soccer, and roundball (a fast, aerobically demanding

game that Tom's students love). All activities are preceded by warm-up stretching and followed by a cool-down period of stretching, and the kids do regular strength training in the weight room all three seasons.

A third element to Tom's program is an "adventure curriculum" with an emphasis on cooperation and group problem solving. Since many of the subjects studied and discussed in health education are "sensitive," private ones, Tom has found that it helps for his students to develop a climate of mutual trust, support, and confidence, and he uses some of the strategies and methods developed by Project Adventure, in Hamilton, Massachusetts, to do that. A few examples of those methods:

▶ *"The Live Wire."* Tom strings a rope between two trees, about five feet off the ground, which represents a live wire that the students have to find a way to get over. They pretend it is a solid wall of electricity, stretching on indefinitely to either side of the trees (so they can't go around it) and into the ground (so they can't go under it). They are given one prop, a two-by-six-by-eight-foot board, and the "problem" is to get the entire group from one side of the wire to the other.

▶ *"Trust Falls."* Each student falls backward off a five-foot platform with eyes closed and is caught by the other students.

▶ *"Blindfold Soccer."* A blindfolded player is verbally directed on getting to the ball and kicking it by his or her "seeing-eye person."

Throughout this innovative and popular class, Tom Walton's primary goal is to increase every student's "R.Q."—or risk quotient. Uniquely, he uses health and fitness education, exercise, and group dynamics to constantly encourage his kids to take physical, emotional, and mental risks without reservations, and to break down whatever barriers they might have that keep them from meeting life head-on and enjoying as much of it as they can.

If you would like to know more about this program, you can write directly to: Tom Walton, Rundlett Junior High School, Smith Street, Concord, NH 03301.

beth kirkpatrick's physical education program, tilford middle school, vinton, iowa

Tom Walton's program is an example of how high-quality physical education can be achieved with a lot of commitment and imagination and very little money. Beth Kirkpatrick, too, has brought tremendous imagination and commitment to her physical education classes at the Tilford Middle School in Vinton, Iowa—but she has also brought to it a *lot* of money. That money was not supplied by the school (which is in a rural town with a population of only five thousand). Beth (a recent junior high physical education "Teacher of the Year") went out and *raised* the money—some two hundred thousand dollars so far in grants and corporate donations—to buy state-of-the-art, high-tech equipment for what is widely thought of as the foremost middle school physical education program in the United States.

Beth team-teaches her forty-five-minute classes with Jim Struve, and every kid in the school is required to take the class every other day. That means that she and Struve are teaching classes that have a minimum of 40 and a maximum of 62 kids in them, for a total of 142 kids each day. These numbers require a lot of inventiveness to keep every student actively involved.

Beth's three principles for operating the program are: every kid in every class is involved to the fullest; all classes are noncompetitive and do nothing that would damage self-esteem; all referees in games are student referees. To insure that everyone is kept active, Beth came up with what she calls the "Ultra Shuffle"—there are only three or four kids on any team at any given time (even football!), and they are constantly shuffled from team to team, so that within the class's twenty minutes of activity or game time, each kid will be on four different teams. In addition to activity time, each class has a warm-up and cool-down period, nine minutes of sustained-heart-rate aerobic activity, and two minutes to discuss the "concept of the day," which can have to do with health, values, stress management, nutrition, and so on. (The kids wear T-shirts or jerseys, created for them by U.S. Games, bearing slogans that coincide with their daily concept, such as: DON'T DO DRUGS and BE FIT. And Beth uses music (mostly classical) and recordings of rain forest and waterfall sounds throughout the class to reduce stress and make the kids feel like they're not in a gym.

But the most innovative element in Beth Kirkpatrick's program is her use of high-tech equipment—equipment usually reserved for college and professional sports programs and adult fitness centers. With the money she has raised from grants and corporate donors, Beth has made the following available to her students:

▶ Thirty pairs of "computer sneakers" (her kids are the only ones in the country using these) that beep every time the foot hits the floor and that measure time and distance traveled and the number of calories burned over a given period.

▶ Nintendo Power Paks that allow kids to run in place on a pad, or pedal on a stationary bike, and their running or biking, along with their speed, is shown on the Nintendo screen. Kids can "run" through an entire Olympic competition and watch their progress as their images actually run across the video screen.

▶ Weight machines especially designed for eleven- through fourteen-year-olds, and a special "Intergalactic Jamball" game using a reduced-height basket so that kids can slam-dunk a "planet" (the ball is a particular planet and the dunker has to do what that planet does: if the dunker knows the planet orbits the sun twice, he has to go in a circle twice before he dunks it—so students are learning about the solar system while playing this kid-size basketball game).

▶ Wristwatch Heart Monitors that the students wear while doing their nine minutes of sustained-heart-rate aerobic exercise. These monitors download heart-rate information for each student onto a computer database, so that complete and accurate records are kept of the entire class's cardiovascular progress. The Tilford Middle School was the first in the country to have and use these heart monitors, thanks to Beth Kirkpatrick's efforts.

If you would like to know more about this program, you can write directly to: Beth Kirkpatrick, Tilford Middle School, Vinton, IA 52349.

At the Tilford Middle School in Vinton, Iowa, and at Rundlett Junior High School in Concord, New Hampshire, two dedicated physical education instructors have created great fitness programs for their students with imagination, resourcefulness, and a bone-deep commitment to the belief that quality PE is important. Those programs should give you an idea of what school physical education *can* be when there is commitment behind it, and also of what it *must* be, nationwide, if we are to permanently turn around America's youth fitness crisis. If the physical education program in your school falls substantially short of these standards, I encourage you and your parents to do what you can to help improve it.

sports participation

Few experiences in your life *can* be as rewarding, as much fun, as educational, and as character-building as participation in sports. At their best, sports teach cooperation, discipline, self-control, timing, how to set and realize goals, and other worthy life lessons. They can build egos, and they can create a deep self-confidence that carries over into other things you do. And finally, learning early to enjoy sports can have the best possible influence on the development of your life-fitness habits by making exercise fun.

On the other side of this coin, few experiences can be as damaging as a bad encounter with sports—as destructive of confidence, as tough on the ego and self-esteem, as unrewarding, as unfun. And such an experience can be, and often is, the *worst possible* influence on the development of good fitness habits by turning kids off exercise and physical activity—sometimes for life. More kids drop out of sports and fitness activity during the years eleven through fourteen than at any other time, and many of those kids never return to physical activity. Quite often it is a bad experience with sports that causes this dropping out.

And who determines which kind of experience *you* will have with sports? It could be a school physical education teacher, a Little League coach, even other kids. But if you are smart, it will be you and only you.

Here are a few tips that might help you make the right decisions about sports participation:

▶ Don't go into a sport only because someone else wants you to participate in it; don't take up a sport for *any* reason other than *you* want to play it or think you might enjoy it.

▶ Many preteens will drop a sport because they find after starting it that they are not yet physically developed enough to compete with kids who entered puberty earlier. Or they may get cut from a team, or feel they are going to be cut, for the same reason. If any of these things happens to you, don't give up on all sports—try taking up another one that, developmentally, you may be more ready to play. A lot of times kids have to try out numerous sports until they find the ones they can perform at well and enjoy.

▶ Don't quit sports because you decide you're just not an athlete. Someone who can't play tennis very well might turn out to be a great swimmer or runner, and someone who can't play basketball well might make a fine soccer player. Almost every kid your age can find a variety of sports at which he or she can excel. It's just a matter of making an effort and believing you can do it.

▶ Before you join a school or community sports program, have a talk with the coach and ask him or her about the issues that concern you. For example, will you get plenty of playing time regardless of how skillful you are at the sport?

▶ Avoid any sports program that puts more emphasis on winning than on everyone's having fun and participating and on good sportsmanship.

▶ Heavy contact sports such as tackle football, lacrosse, and ice hockey can be especially dangerous for boys during puberty.

▶ Girls and boys should not play on the same sports teams after about age twelve or thirteen.

▶ Cardiorespiratory endurance becomes trainable and really improvable for the first time between eleven and fifteen, so this is a great time to take up one of the "aerobic" sports, such as cross-country running, swimming, bike racing, or rowing.

▶ Regardless of whether or not you are playing a school or community team sport, this is also an ideal time in your life to take up one or more of the lifetime fitness activities—which can also be sports—such as tennis, alpine and cross-country skiing, skating, or canoeing.

▶ If for some reason you can't or don't want to be involved in intramural or interscholastic school sports, look into what your community has to offer. You can probably find classes for kids your age in the martial arts and various kinds of dance, including

aerobic dance. Little League and youth programs in hockey, soccer, and football are common almost everywhere; and many YMCAs, YWCAs, and city Departments of Parks and Recreation offer excellent programs in swimming, wrestling, track and field, basketball, soccer, gymnastics, tennis, volleyball, aerobics, and martial arts. Access to many of these programs is usually surprisingly inexpensive (a typical teenage YMCA membership, for example, costs seventy dollars a year). As with school programs, you should talk with the instructor or coach *before* joining a community sports program to get the answers to any questions you might have.

Finally, though the right kinds of organized sports programs in school or in the community can—like school physical education—contribute to the development of good lifetime exercise habits, they are not crucial to that development. If you do wind up dropping out of sports, or if you never take them up, that's okay, as long as you don't let it stop you from doing other forms of exercise, like the ones in this book, that will help you to get fit and to stay that way. Lifetime fitness is what you're after. That's the prize, and if you put this book to good use, you will never have to depend on sports to win it.

Good luck!

the twenty-second chin-up

The last time I saw Franz Steeger was one of the most important days of my life. It was in the summer after the soccer game that Annaliese had played in, and I was fourteen.

I had been interested in making myself into some kind of athlete ever since the day I had seen Franz with his shirt off at the quarry when I was eleven. For the past year and a half I had started experimenting with different kinds of training—doing aerobics and skill training with my friend Siggy, and doing flexibility and strength training on my own at home and down at the lake during the summer.

The lake was only about a hundred yards from my house, and it was private, which meant that people had to pay to use it. On weekends during the summer, thousands of people would come from Graz to swim and lie on the sand and grass. I had learned to swim in this lake when I was six, so I knew every inch of it and I loved the place, even though it was swampy and muddy and no one ever cut the tall grass surrounding it. My friends and I grew up having swimming races in the lake, playing water tag, and having monstrous mud fights all summer long.

But the thing I liked best about the lake was that it was where all the older boys who were athletes in training hung out. There was a swimming instructor named Sepp who appeared one summer and brought with him all of his friends from Graz. These guys were all working out—throwing the javelin, boxing, and wrestling—over on the north shore of the lake  around a small campground. Sig and I used to ride our bicycles over there and watch them when we were younger. But the summer we were fourteen, we were already in pretty good shape ourselves, and we started hanging around with the group on the north shore, even though all of them were older than we were, some by three or four years. After a while they sort of accepted us, though, and Sig and I joined right into all the activities.

The two of us felt we were in heaven. It was like the days of the gladiators or the ancient Olympics, spending our time wrestling and boxing, shotputting, swimming, throwing the javelin, doing push-ups, and doing chin-ups on a tree limb. At night some of the older guys would bring their girlfriends down to the campground, and we would cook meat and vegetables over a fire as though we were a tribe of hunters.

Two or three times early in the summer, Siggy and I tried to convince our friend Annaliese to come down to the campground with us, but she always said no. When we asked her why not, she would blush and just say she was busy. After a while we got so caught up in our life on the lake that we stopped asking her.

Franz Steeger showed up once or twice early in the summer, but did not appear again until the very end. No one could understand Franz's absence, because he had been like the leader of the north shore group— the fastest swimmer, the best shotputter, javelin thrower, and wrestler, and by far the strongest. The summer before, he had been at the lake every day, training for the Austrian national shotput team, which most people believed he would make by the following year. Then all of a sudden, that summer, he just stopped coming down to train, and no one knew why.

At the campground was a big tree with a limb that stuck straight out, parallel to the ground, and was just low enough so that you could grab it if you jumped. We used this branch for doing chin-ups. The branch was huge, so you couldn't close your fingers around it and your fingers would usually tire out before your arm muscles did. It was hard to do even five chin-ups on this branch. But the summer before, Franz Steeger had done twenty-one, and that was a record that no one else had even come close to, though some very good athletes and very strong guys had tried to break it.

I decided early in the summer that I would do everything I could to break Franz's chin-up record. I didn't tell anyone but Sig and my brother, Meinhard, what I wanted to do, and even they laughed and said I didn't have a chance. But I had already learned that you can do almost anything you want to do in life if you work hard enough at it, and I was determined to give it my best shot.

I tried the branch for the first time in late June right after Sig and I started hanging out on the north shore, and I could only do seven chin-ups, even though I thought I was pretty strong. When I dropped off the branch my fingers were so cramped, I couldn't close them. Meinhard told me that if I wanted to improve, I would have to strengthen my fingers as well as my arm and shoulder muscles, and that he would show me how to do that. Meinhard had once done fifteen chin-ups on the branch, the third most ever done, so I listened to him.

For the rest of the summer, everywhere I went, I carried two tennis balls, one in each pocket, and I was constantly squeezing them. I even got to the point where I *dreamed* about squeezing those tennis balls. I also did lots of other arm and shoulder exercises, and I spent a half hour every day chinning on the branch. After the first week of this, my fingers were all cut and bloody from the bark; and by the second week, I had to wrap them in gauze. But gradually my fingers got tougher and stronger, and the number of chin-ups I could do began to creep up. By mid-July I could do twelve, and then fifteen by the first of August. It took me a full two more weeks to get up to eighteen, and then for some reason, I couldn't do any more, no matter how hard I trained. The summer was nearly over and I was stuck at eighteen. That was more than anyone but Franz had ever done, and Meinhard and Sig both told me I should be happy and proud with what I had accomplished after only one summer's training, and that the next year I would surely break Franz's record. I listened to them, but I still wanted to break it that year. I wanted it badly.

The weekend before we had to go back to school, there was a big party and barbecue at the campground. One of Sepp's friends, who was a butcher in Graz, brought out a whole pig and roasted it over the fire, and there were the usual games and competitions going on. I had been swim-

ming all day and had not done my chin-up training yet. I was sitting on a log and talking with Sig and Meinhard when Meinhard said, "Look, there's Franz Steeger."

And it was. He was getting off his motorcycle. He looked a good bit thinner than he had at the beginning of the summer.

Franz walked into the group around the fire and everyone was very glad to see him. It seemed like everyone there was trying to shake his hand at the same time. Then after a few minutes of talking to some of the kids around the fire, he walked over to us.

"Meinhard, Arnold, and Sig —how *are* you?" he said in his deep voice and shook each of our hands. He was as loud and cheerful as always, but at the same time something about him seemed changed.

Just then Sepp, the swimming instructor, came over and clapped me on the shoulder. "Arnold has been working all summer on his chin-ups to try and break your record," he told Franz.

I was very embarrassed.

I hadn't even realized that Sepp *knew* what I was doing.

Franz stared at me thoughtfully for a moment. "Can you do it?" he asked.

"I don't know. Not yet. I've gotten up to eighteen, but I can't seem to go any further."

Franz grinned. "You do the rest with your mind," he said.

"What?" I asked him.

"Come here a moment and let's talk," he said. He took my arm and led me away from the others. I didn't know what to expect, but I was hoping Franz wasn't angry.

"Listen," he said. "My father died this summer, and I now have to support my mother, brother, and sister. I've taken a job working in a garage. It's a good job, but I no longer have time for training. Training is finished for me. The shotput is finished." He looked me in the eyes again, as if he were thinking of something a long way off. "Do you know why I'm telling you all this?"

"No," I said, "but I am very sorry to hear it."

Franz shrugged. "I have been watching you for a number of years and you not only have a strong body, but a strong mind. You will do whatever you want to do, believe me. I would like to see you leave this small place and go out into the world and become a famous athlete, and I know you can do that. *If* you do it, you would be doing it for me as well as for yourself . . . you would be doing it for all of us here. Do you understand what I am saying?"

"Yes," I said, though I wasn't sure that I did.

Franz grinned at me. "Now go do twenty-two chin-ups. Not one less."

We started to walk back to the tree, but he stopped me again and said, "Arnold, there is one more thing. Annaliese and I are seeing each other. We are dating. I hope you aren't unhappy with that. She hopes so, too."

Now it was my turn to grin. "I am *very* happy about that," I told him.

We walked together over to the chin-up tree and without saying anything to anyone, I dried my hands on my pants and jumped up and grabbed the limb. It felt like shaking hands with an old friend. I did the chin-ups slowly, clearing my chin well over the branch on each one and keeping my breathing regular and deep as I had learned to do. By the time I reached twelve or thirteen, it looked like everyone at the party had gathered around the tree and was listening to Franz count off the chin-ups. I got to seventeen without even tiring. Eighteen was hard, but I did the nineteenth, the one I had been chasing for weeks. Then I thought I was finished, and I just hung from the branch looking up at it, wishing but not really believing that I could do three more.

"Now you do it with your mind, Arnold," said Franz quietly. I have thought of that many times since. Whenever I have been faced with something I thought I couldn't do in life, I have heard Franz Steeger's calm voice say, "Now you do it with your mind, Arnold."

I hung from the branch and thought of how Franz would never make the national shotput team now, and I thought of Annaliese and how her voice had gone quiet the first time she ever spoke to Franz. And then I thought of nothing else but the branch and of getting my chin over it three more times.

"Twenty . . . twenty-one," counted Franz, his voice growing excited. And as I pulled my chin up toward the branch for the last time, just before all the shouting and clapping broke out and Franz carried me around the roasting pig on his shoulders, I thought, with so much joy that it felt as though I might break open with laughter: he's right, Franz is *right*—I can become whatever I want to become.

And what did Franz become? Well, he was right when he told me he was finished with shotputting, but he went on to become a very successful businessman, owning two or three garages in Graz. He and Annaliese got married and had four children, and Franz coaches soccer and shotputting on the weekends. He is much loved and respected by all the young athletes in Graz.

outline of appendixes

APPENDIX a

aerobic exercises and activities

a. tips

If you do nothing else for your fitness program, you should do some kind of aerobic activity at least three times a week for twenty-five minutes, preferably every other day. Here are some tips on how to perform the various aerobic activities I recommend and how to do warm-up and cool-down:

▶ When you first start doing the aerobic part of your program, you may find that you can't exercise at all without getting too tired. That's okay. If you find, for example, that you can't run for twenty-five minutes straight, run for as long as you can (and still talk), and then walk briskly for the rest of the time. As the running gets easier for you (and it will), run for a longer period of time and walk less. When you're running slowly for the entire twenty-five minutes and *that* gets easy, run faster. Just listen to your body, and it will tell you when you are exercising hard enough (to be good for you) but not too hard.

▶ It is very important that your aerobic exercise or play be done *continuously* (without stopping) for twenty-five minutes. You *can* combine exercises by going from one to another during the twenty-five minutes, as long as you don't stop for more than a few seconds between them. For example, you could run for ten minutes, then immediately do fifteen minutes of calisthenics, for as good a workout as twenty-five minutes of either of those two exercises would give you. What's important is to get your heart rate up to your target rate and keep it there for twenty-five minutes.

▶ You should always warm up before your aerobic workout and cool down after it. I recommend five minutes of warm-up and five minutes of cool-down. Warm up with walking, walking in a circle, calisthenics, jumping jacks, or with some of the stretching exercises in Appendix B. The best way to cool down is to walk slowly for two or three minutes after your exercise, and then do some simple stretching exercises. The point of warming up is to prepare your muscles and heart for vigorous exercise, and the cool-down is to bring your body back down safely and slowly from hard work to rest (*rest* meaning normal activity, not actually lying down). Both are *very important*, so don't try to save a little time by skipping them.

▶ If you are a good bit overweight, running is probably not the best aerobic exercise for you to begin your program with. Try brisk walking, swimming, or cycling instead. When your fitness and nutrition program brings your weight down close to normal, you can begin running if you'd like.

▶ If you are going to run for your aerobic exercise, get a good pair of running shoes, and run so that each foot lands gently on its heel, then rolls forward onto the ball of the foot before pushing off. Running on your toes can give you leg cramps and can stress the lower leg.

▶ If you decide to swim for your workout, swim laps. You may find it difficult at first to swim for the entire twenty-five minutes. If so, alternate swimming with short "breaks" of treading water, floating, etc. Gradually, cut down on the breaks until you are swimming slowly for twenty-five minutes, then increase your speed. To get the maximum aerobic benefit from swimming, you have to swim properly. If you like swimming but don't do it well, take some lessons.

▶ If you decide to walk for your aerobic workout, do it *briskly*. Inhale and exhale with deep breaths, take long, comfortable strides (but don't overstride), and swing your arms energetically. It may take you a few minutes of walking, even briskly, to get your heartbeat to its target rate; if so, allow a little more than the allotted twenty-five minutes for your walking workouts.

▶ If you decide to bike for your aerobic workout, do it *safely,* and always wear a helmet. You should try for a brisk, consistent pedaling cadence (not pedaling fast downhill and slow uphill). Start at around sixty to seventy pedal revolutions per minute and try to work up to one hundred or so. Road biking, mountain biking, and BMX can all provide good workouts. (So can a stationary bike.) Start your program by biking slowly for five minutes, then working up to your target heart rate. As you get in better shape, you can go more quickly to your target heart rate. To get maximum benefit and enjoyment from biking, your bike should "fit" you. If you're not sure whether it fits you, take it into a bicycle shop and let them assist you. (Remember, always wear your helmet when you ride your bicycle.)

b. list of exercises and activities

The following will benefit you aerobically when done on a continuous basis, without stopping, for at least twenty-five minutes at a time. It doesn't matter which aerobic activities you pick for your workouts, as long as you do them as scheduled and do them vigorously enough so that your heartbeat is sustained at your target rate. I recommend that you learn to enjoy as many of these activities as possible to provide yourself with a good variety for your aerobic workouts.

the big four
Brisk Walking
Jogging and Running
Bicycling
Swimming

other great aerobic exercises
Aerobic Classes
Step Aerobics
Aerobic Dance
Cross-Country Skiing
Rowing

activities and sports that can be aerobic if done continuously
Jumping Rope
Skating (Ice or Roller)
Soccer or Lacrosse
Handball or Racquetball
Tennis, Squash, Badminton
Canoeing
Mountain Climbing

The following is a table, adapted from Dr. Ken Cooper's *Kid Fitness,* which lays out a ten-week walk/jog program for kids who might want a structured aerobic program that brings them along slowly and safely. This is an excellent program with which to begin your aerobic workouts.

c. walk/jog time chart for boys and girls ages eleven to fourteen

week	activity	distance (miles)	time goal (minutes) girls	boys	times/week
1	W	2.0	34.00	32.00	3
2	W	2.5	42:00	40:00	3
3	W/J	2.0	28:00	26:00	3
4	W/J	2.0	26:00	24:00	3
5	J	2.0	24:00	22:00	3
6	J	2.0	22:00	20:00	3
7	J	2.5	27:00	25:00	3
8	J	2.5	25:00	23:00	3
9	J	3.0	33:00	30:00	3
10	J	3.0	<30:00	<27:00	3

KEY: W = WALK; J = JOG; < = LESS THAN

(NOTE: To help you read this chart, if you are a boy, in week 1 of your program, you would walk 2 miles in 32 minutes or less 3 days a week. If you are a girl, in week 6 of your program, you would jog 2 miles, 3 days a week, and try to do it in 22 minutes or less.)

APPENDIX B

flexibility exercises

a. tips

Here are some important tips on how to do your stretching exercises:

▶ Start your stretching with range-of-motion or "limbering up" stretches. This will warm up your muscles for muscle stretching.

▶ The proper way to do a muscle stretch is to stretch out the muscle slowly (*no bouncing, ever!*) until you feel a mild tug of tension in it. Relax and hold that position for five seconds, then stretch the muscle a little further until you feel another tug. Now hold that position for as long as the exercise calls for. Breathe slowly and deeply as you stretch, and don't hold your breath. Never bounce, and never force a muscle to stretch to the point of pain.

▶ When you first begin stretching, count to yourself the seconds you hold each stretch— this will insure that you hold it long enough.

▶ Don't stretch very sore or injured muscles. If you have an injured or sore muscle, massage it daily and give it time to heal before stretching it.

▶ Make sure you stretch in a warm room or place.

▶ Take your time. Don't hurry your stretching, just enjoy the nice easy way it makes your body feel when you are finished.

▶ For the flexibility segment of your program, you should do at least one stretch for each body part given here. You should do extra stretches for any muscle and/or joint you are about to exercise strenuously—the legs before running, for example—or for muscles that are tight.

b. list of flexibility exercises

neck stretches

1. Chin Stretch

Sit in a chair with back straight. Now jut your chin out and down, curling it into your chest gently and slowly, hold for three seconds, and then come out of that tuck and point your chin as far up toward the sky as you can, holding for three seconds. You will feel this stretch in the back of the neck and in the throat area. Do this upward and downward stretch ten to fifteen times.

2. Neck-to-Shoulder Stretch

Sit in a chair with back straight. Tilt head to the left, at the same time pulling down with your right shoulder to maximize the stretch. Do the same, tilting your head to the right and pulling down with the left shoulder. Hold on each side for three to five seconds and release. This is to be done smoothly and slowly. Do this ten times on each side.

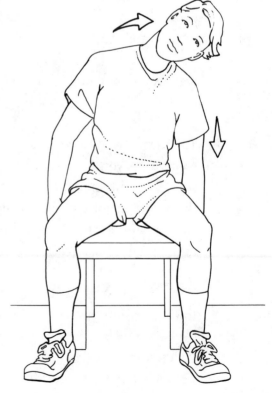

3. Head Turns

Stand or sit for this exercise with back straight. Now turn your head to the right as far as you can and hold for three to five seconds. Turn your head to the left and do the same. Do this ten times on each side.

shoulder stretches

4. Two-Part Arm and Shoulder Stretch

With both arms held overhead, gently pull the elbow of your right arm behind your head with your left hand, letting your forearm and hand hang down your back, until you feel the stretch in your shoulder and the back of your arm. Hold for ten seconds. Then pull your right elbow *across* your chest toward your left shoulder as far as it will comfortably go and hold that stretch for ten seconds. Now do the same two stretches with your left arm.

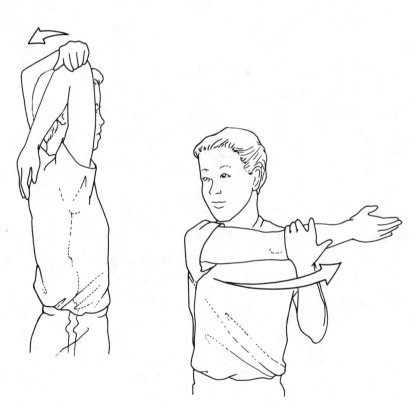

5. Shoulder Circles

Stand with arms at sides and circle one shoulder forward, then the other, and keep circling for one minute. Now reverse and circle shoulders backward for one minute.

arm stretches

6. Arm Circles

This exercise increases range of motion as well as stretches the muscles. Stand with feet shoulder-width apart, arms held straight out at sides at about shoulder height, palms down. Slowly start working your hands forward in a small circular motion and gradually increase the size of the circle until finally your arms are reaching their complete range of motion. Now change directions and circle your hands backward, gradually making the circle smaller and smaller until your arms are back at the starting position. Do this for one minute in each direction.

7. Arms, Shoulder, and Chest Stretch

Interlace your fingers behind your back and lift both arms behind you until you feel a stretch in your arms, shoulders, and chest. Keep your chest out and your chin in. Hold for ten seconds.

8. Arms and Upper-Back Stretch

Interlace your fingers over your head and face your palms upward. Push your arms up and back until you feel a stretch in your upper back and the backs of your arms. Hold for ten seconds.

chest stretches

9. Pectoral Reaches

This is a great exercise for dancers or for anyone who wants to improve his or her posture. Stand with feet shoulder-width apart, arms raised with elbows bent slightly and held just below shoulder level. Pull your stomach in and pinch your buttocks together as if you're wearing a clothespin. Now lift your ribcage slightly and extend forward the right side of your chest, then bring it back in. Do the same with the left side of the chest. Do this fifteen times on both sides.

back stretches

10. Side and Back Sretch

Extend both your arms over your head and clap your hands together. Bend slowly to the right, using your right hand to pull your left arm over your head and down toward the ground, until you feel a stretch from the back of your arm down through your side and spine. Don't overstretch—just go as far as is comfortable, and hold for six seconds. Now do the same on your left side.

11. Back Stretch

Lie flat on your back. Grasp your right knee with both hands and pull it up and in toward your chest as far as is comfortable. Hold it there for ten seconds, keeping your head flat on the floor. Then do the same thing with your left leg. Then pull both knees into your chest and hold them there for ten seconds. Repeat the sequence three times.

12. Upper-Back and Neck Stretch

Standing up, lace your fingers behind your head and slowly pull your head forward and down toward your chest until you feel a stretch at the back of your neck. Hold for five seconds. Do this stretch three times, holding each for five seconds.

13. Groin and Lower-Back Stretch

A great stretch to do before strenuous exercise. Sit on the floor and put the soles of your feet together in front of you. Holding on to your toes, gently lean forward from the hips until you feel a stretch in your groin and lower back. Don't push your head and shoulders forward to initiate the stretch, but lean forward *from the hips*. If you have a problem leaning forward, move your feet farther out in front of you. Hold the stretch for fifteen seconds, relax, and do it two more times for fifteen seconds apiece.

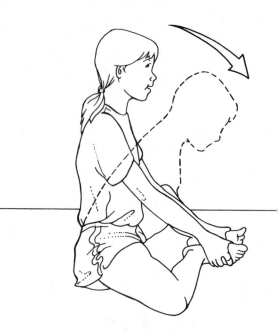

thigh stretches

14. Hamstring and Hip Stretch

Sitting on the floor with your legs slightly bent at the knees, grasp your calves and slide your hands forward toward your ankles as far as you can comfortably go. Hold the stretch for ten seconds. (Remember, don't bounce.)

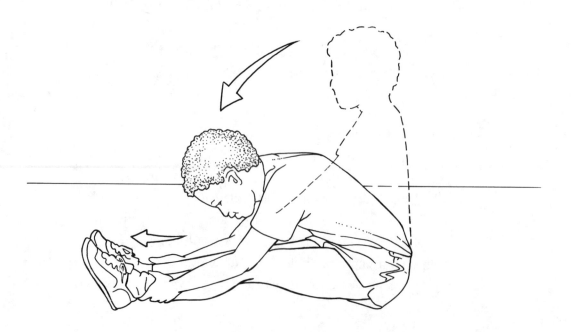

15. Thigh and Knee Stretch

Stand a few inches from a wall and put your right hand on the wall. Hold the top of your right foot in your left hand and gently pull your heel up toward your buttocks. Hold for thirty seconds, then reverse your position and stretch the left thigh and knee.

16. Hamstring (Back of the Thigh) Stretch

A good advanced stretch for running, biking, and sports. Sit with the sole of your left foot touching the inside of your right thigh. Your right leg should be straight out, with the foot upright. Now slowly bend forward from the hips toward your right foot, sliding your hands down your right leg to the ankle, until you feel a slight stretch in the back of your right leg. Don't push your head forward as you bend into the stretch. Hold that position for ten seconds, then bend a little more forward from the hips until you feel another tug. Hold that final position for fifteen more seconds. Then reverse your position and do the same stretch with the left leg.

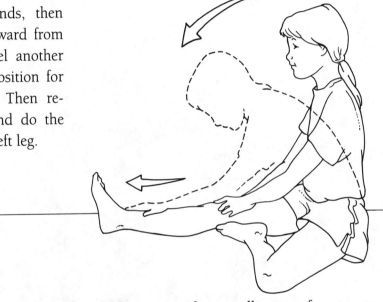

calf stretches

17. Calf Stretch

Stand six to ten inches from a wall and lean on it with your elbows or forearms. Rest your head on your hands. Bend the knee of your forward leg and stretch the other leg out behind you as far as you can and still keep your heel on the ground. Hold the stretch for ten seconds. Then stretch the other leg.

18. Calf/Foot Stretch

Sit on the floor with arms at your sides, legs together straight out in front of you, back straight. Flex toes of feet up toward your head and hold for three seconds, then tilt feet out to the sides till your littlest toes touch the floor, and then slowly point toes back toward the floor, working through the balls of your feet. This exercise should be done very slowly and smoothly. You will also feel a nice stretch in the front of the leg as you point your toes back toward the floor. Do this twenty times.

entire body stretch

19.

Lie flat on your back with your legs two or three inches apart and your arms lying over your head, also two or three inches apart. Now stretch your arms out in the direction in which they are pointing and, at the same time, stretch your feet in the opposite direction, as if you were trying to lengthen your body. Hold for five seconds, then relax. Repeat three or four times.

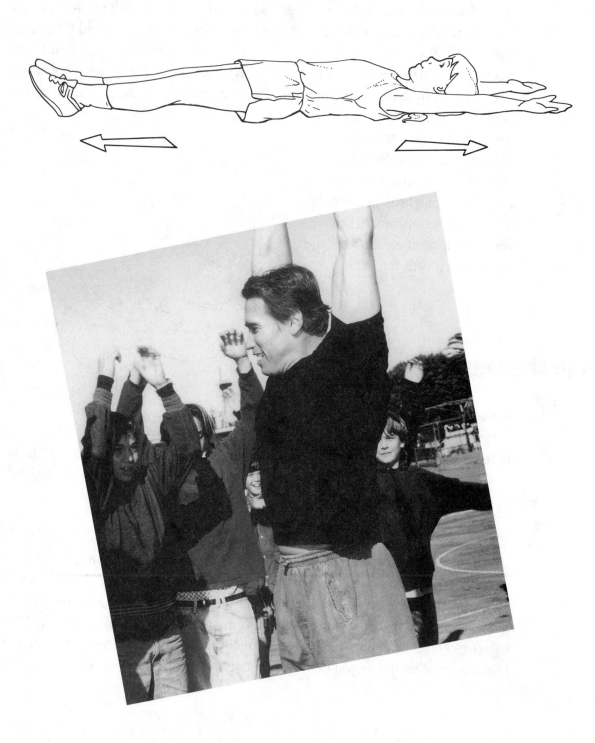

APPENDIX C

muscular strength and endurance exercises

a. tips

Here are some important tips on how to do your strength training:

▶ I recommend that you do at least one exercise from each of the muscle groups every time you do your strength workout (that is, one exercise for stomach, one for legs, one for chest, etc.). After a while, you'll probably want to do two or three exercises per muscle group. Start with one set of as many repetitions as you can comfortably do for each exercise, and as you get stronger, increase the repetitions and go to two and then three sets for each exercise. (A *repetition* is one performance of the exercise—for example, a single situp; a *set* is a group of repetitions done without stopping.) You should rest for twenty to thirty seconds between sets.

▶ It is important to breathe properly during resistance exercise—exhale on the exertion phase (when your muscle contracts) and inhale on the relaxation phase (when your muscle relaxes). During a push-up, for example, exhale as you're pushing up and inhale as you let your body down.

▶ Never push a muscle to the point where it hurts. Take it easy and increase your reps gradually. If and when fatigue causes you to change your form for doing the exercise, stop.

▶ You should begin your program with one or more of the easier exercises for each body part and move on to more difficult exercises for each body part as those muscles get stronger. Don't be surprised if certain of your muscles get stronger sooner than others, and don't push too fast toward doing the more advanced exercises. A good rule of thumb is that you are ready to move on to a more advanced exercise when you can easily do two sets of twenty repetitions of the exercise you are currently doing.

▶ Concentrate on each exercise. This is one of the secrets of productive resistance training —*think* about the muscles you are working and concentrate on doing the exercise properly.

▶ Don't expect your muscles to get big from the exercises given here unless you've reached puberty. But your muscle strength and endurance *will* improve from the exercises in this book, and that is what is important for your health and for sports performance.

▶ As with all forms of exercise, the key to getting real benefits from strength training is *regularity*. Pick a time—two days a week (not in a row)—when it is convenient for you to do your thirty-five minutes of stretching and strength exercises, and try to do them at that time *every* week without missing. One advantage these exercises have over weight training is that they are portable—you can do them at camp, at a friend's house, anywhere.

▶ If a particular muscle group gets sore from your training, exercise other muscle groups until the soreness goes away. Don't try to strength-train a sore muscle or muscle group.

▶ Try to do each and every exercise perfectly. By making sure that each individual exercise is done properly in an entire set, you will maximize the benefit your body is getting from that entire set.

▶ If you have a particular body part weaker than the others, spend more time training it.

b. list of exercises

stomach, waist, and leg exercises

1. Bent-Leg Sit-Ups

Sitting on the floor with your knees bent, place your feet under some stationary object. Cross your arms over your chest, with your hands on your shoulders. Now lower your upper body until your lower back touches the floor, and sit back up for one repetition. Do these slowly and fluidly (don't jerk your upper body upward). Do as many repetitions as you comfortably can, and increase your repetitions as the exercise gets easier for you, working up to forty to fifty. For an easier version of this exercise, don't lower your upper body as much.

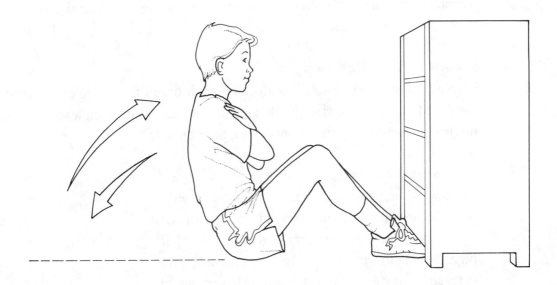

2. Crunches

This is a great waist toner. Lie on your back, legs bent at the knees and elevated, with your feet stationary against an object or wall. Put your hands on your hips, lift your shoulders from the floor and roll them forward so that your chin touches your chest, and "crunch," or tense, your stomach muscles. Hold the crunch for a count of three, then relax back to your initial position for one repetition. Work up to fifty of these in a set.

3. Leg Ins

Lie flat on the floor with your hands underneath your buttocks. Holding your legs together, with knees bent, raise them six inches off the floor. Bring your knees in toward your chest as far as you can, then straighten your legs slowly for one repetition. Work up to twenty-five to thirty repetitions.

4. Side Bends I

Stand with arms at your sides, back straight, and reach down one side of your body with your hand along your outer thigh, thus stretching the muscles on the opposite side of your waist. Alternate twenty repetitions to each side.

5. Standing Twists

Stand with feet shoulder-width apart and arms raised out to the sides at shoulder level. With arms straight and hips kept facing forward, turn to the left so that you are looking over your left shoulder and feel a pull in your waist. Hold for three seconds and come back to center. Now turn to the right and do the same. Do these twenty times on each side.

6. Standing Side Reaches

Same as above, except instead of turning, you lean out to your left with arms held at shoulder level and kept straight, then come back to center, then lean out to the right and back to center. Do this twenty times on each side.

7. Side Bends II

Stand with feet hip-width apart and arms at your sides. Raise your right arm straight up toward the sky as you lower your left arm down the outer left thigh, leaning toward the left. Your right arm should be reaching upward as your left arm is lowering. Do the same on the right side. Do these twenty times on each side.

8. Seated Twists

These are good for strengthening the side muscles of the waist (intercostals and obliques), and also for increasing spinal flexibility. Sit on a bench, stool, or chair and hold your arms out by your sides at shoulder level. Twist at the waist to your right, bringing your arms and upper body around as far as they will comfortably go. Then come back through your starting position and twist in the other direction. Alternate twenty-five repetitions to each side. This is also a great warm-up exercise.

9. Aided Knee Bends

You will need a bureau and a chair or stool for this exercise. Stand in front of the chair and hold on to the bureau at about waist height. With your back straight, lower your buttocks to the seat of the chair, then stand back up slowly and smoothly and feel the front muscles of the upper thigh working. Do this twenty times.

10. Knee Bends

You will need a chair for this exercise. Stand facing the back of the chair and use it for balance by gently holding on to the back. With feet six inches apart, back straight, using your legs only, slowly lower yourself toward the floor until your thighs are almost parallel with it, and then stand smoothly back up again (do not jump or use the chair to pull yourself up) in one fluid motion for one rep. You should feel this exercise in the quadriceps muscles at the front of the thighs. Work up to twenty repetitions per set.

11. Side Leg Raises

Lie on your left side on the floor, head supported by left hand with right hand resting on floor in front of chest for balance, and legs straight with toes together. Lift top (or right) leg up so that toe is pointed toward ceiling, while bottom leg stays straight and flat on the floor. Now lower the leg back down slowly to complete one rep. Do this fifteen to twenty times with each leg for one set.

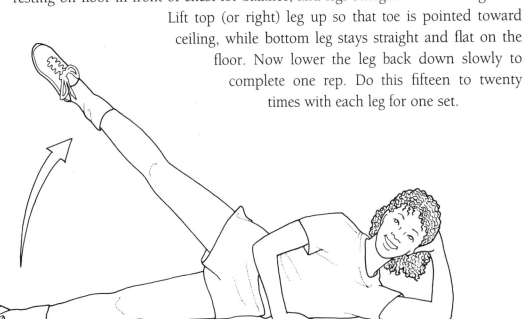

12. Calf Raises

Find a thick book or piece of four-by-four-inch board. Stand on it, with your feet a few inches apart, so that only the balls of your feet and the first couple of inches of your instep are on the object and your heels are dropped down as far as they will go. It helps to have something in front of you to hold on to. Now stand up slowly on the balls of your feet until your calf muscles contract fully. Hold that position for a count of five—feeling the contraction in your calves—then let your heels drop back down slowly to their original position for one repetition. Work up to twenty-five repetitions, held for five seconds each. This exercise can also be done one leg at a time, which makes it harder.

13. Step-Ups

Find a sturdy stool, bench, or box about the same height as a stairway step, and stand in front of it. Step up on the object with your right foot (*step*, don't heave or jump up—let your thigh muscles bring you up). Now step down and step back up with your left foot. Step down again for one repetition with each foot. Work up to thirty to forty step-ups with each foot. This is good for both the frontal thigh muscles and the buttocks, and is also a great aerobic exercise.

14. Lunges

Lunges strengthen the upper legs and hips and also improve balance and hip flexibility. Stand with your feet together and your arms held straight out to your sides for balance. Now step forward two or three feet with your right leg and sink onto it until you touch the knee of your left leg to the floor (if this is hard, don't sink so far). Come back up to your original position for one repetition with that leg. Now do the same thing on your left leg. Alternate legs up to twenty-five lunges per leg.

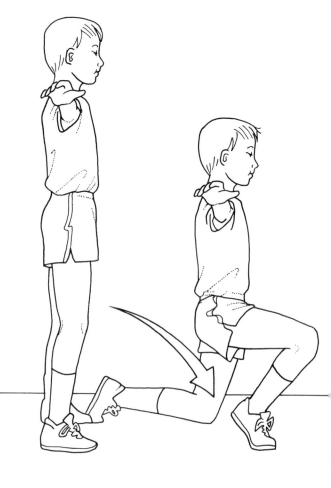

15. Wall Squats

A great exercise for building up the endurance of the big quadriceps muscle of the thigh, and for many sports, particularly skiing. Stand with your back flat against the wall, your feet shoulder-width apart. Slide your back down the wall, and walk your feet out until your thighs form a ninety-degree angle with the wall and your calves a ninety-degree angle with the floor. Your feet should still be shoulder-width apart. Fold your arms over your chest. Now squat there for as long as you can. Try to add five seconds to how long you hold the squat each time you do the exercise. Do one set per workout.

16. Lying Rear-Leg Raises

Lie on your stomach on a flat surface, up on your elbows with arms shoulder-width apart. Slowly lift (do not jerk) one leg completely off the floor, trying to keep it relatively straight, then lower back down. Now do the same with the other leg. Do this twenty times with each leg. If you have lower-back problems, don't do this exercise.

17. Leg Raises on All Fours

Get down on all fours with hands and knees on floor about shoulder-width apart. Bring your head down toward your chest as you bring your right knee in to your stomach. Now stretch your leg back out, straightening and extending it as far upward as you can, as you bring your head back up and stretch your chin upward. Now do the same with the left leg. Do this twenty times with each leg. This exercise works on the abdominals, neck, and chest muscles as well as the legs and hips.

upper body exercises

18. Table Push-Offs

This is a beginner's form of push-ups. Stand in front of a table, bench, dresser—something about half your height—with your feet two to three feet away and a foot apart. Put your hands on the table a little wider than shoulder-width apart. Hold your back straight and lower your body so that your chest touches the object, then push back up for one repetition. Work up to twenty-five to thirty repetitions.

19. Bent Knee Push-Ups (Easy)

If you can't do the exercise below, substitute this one. With your chin to the floor and hands and knees holding your weight, push your body up until arms and back are straight, then lower yourself back down until chin touches floor. Do this as many times as you can at first and work up to twenty-five reps.

20. Push-Ups (Harder)

This is the traditional push-up exercise, and you begin it by lying flat on your stomach, with your feet on their toes and with your hands on a level with your chest and directly under your shoulders. Lift your midsection off the floor, until only your chest is touching, and then push up until your arms are fully extended, keeping your head down and your back straight. Lower yourself until your chest is touching the floor again for one repetition. Work up to twenty-five reps. Each time you do push-ups, try to do one more.

21. Prone Flies

Lying on your back, knees bent, hold objects of equal weight in both hands with arms outstretched on either side. Now raise the two objects together over the chest until they barely touch, then lower arms back down until they rest on the floor again. Work up to twenty reps.

22. Alternate Flies and Pull-Overs with Books

A good exercise for strengthening the chest and upper abdominals, and also for upper-body flexibility. Lie on your back on the floor, knees bent, holding two books of equal weight (or soup cans, etc.) directly over your chest. With your arms slightly bent, lower the books out to the sides to the floor, then bring your arms back up in a slight bow, as though you were hugging something, until the books touch. Then, with the books together, lower your arms back behind your head to the floor and, using your chest and upper stomach muscles, pull your arms back up to a vertical position for one full repetition of the exercise. Try to do the four movements smoothly and at the maximum stretch. As you get stronger, you can use heavier books. Work up to twenty reps.

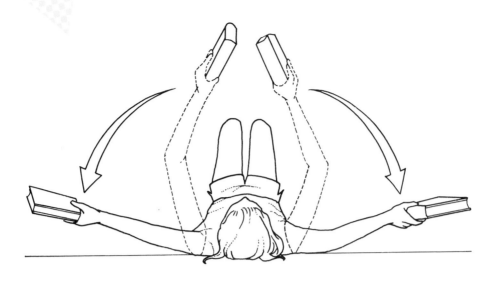

23. Suspended Push-Ups

This is a more difficult version of the normal push-up. Get three chairs—one for your feet and one for each hand. Assume the push-up position on these chairs as if you were on the floor. The push-up will vary in that your body will be lowered slightly below the level of the chair seats before pushing up. Lower your body smoothly as far down as you can, then push back up for one rep. Do as many of these as you can, and try to work up to twenty reps. This is an advanced exercise and careful attention must be paid to setting up the chairs securely.

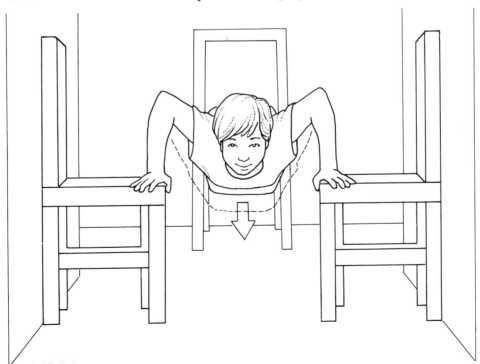

back exercises

24. Lower-Back Extensions

This exercise strengthens the lower-back muscles and buttocks, and is also good for lower-back flexibility. Lie on your stomach and chest with your head held off the floor, your feet against something that won't move, and your hands held together at the small of your back. Arching at the waist, lift your head and chest upward as far as you comfortably can, hold them there for a count of three, then slowly lower back to your original position for one repetition. Work up to ten reps. Adults with lower-back problems should be careful with this exercise.

25. Lat Pulls

Lat is short for latissimus dorsi, the back muscles that this exercise works. Stand in front of something solid like a post and grip it at chest height. Keep your feet about a foot from the object and a bit more than shoulder-width apart. Lean back, fully extending your arms, then pull yourself to the post, touching your chest. Pull with your *back,* not your arms. Work up to fifteen repetitions per set.

26. Modified Pull-Ups

To do these great back pull-ups, you will need a couple of stable objects about two feet high—a couple of chairs or tables—and a broomstick or some other kind of sturdy pole. Arrange the pole as shown in the illustration. Make sure the pole is firmly in place. Lie on your back and take a wide grip on the pole. Keeping your heels on the floor, pull your chest as close as you can to the pole, then let yourself down slowly for one repetition. Keep your back straight as you do these and let your back muscles do the pulling. Work up to ten repetitions.

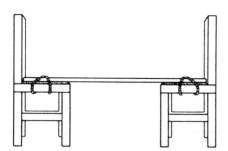

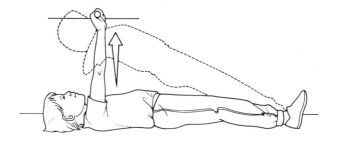

shoulder exercises

27. Shoulder Flies with Books

Stand with feet shoulder-width apart, arms at your sides, holding two books of equal weight and size. Raise your arms up to shoulder level with palms facing down holding the books. Hold this position as long as you can and then drop slowly. Rest five seconds, then raise the books again and hold. Remember, hold as long as you can each time until the ache becomes just about painful, then drop, but always try to raise your arms up one more time before ending your set. Work up to twenty repetitions, and when the exercise gets easy for you, use heavier books.

28. Push-Offs

Stand with feet a little farther than shoulder-width apart facing a sturdy object, such as a table (preferably something a little shorter than waist height), and place your hands on the object. Hands should be placed a little farther apart than your shoulders, to allow you to bend toward the object fully. Bend forward so that your back is flat, and lean in toward the object until the top of your head is in line with your wrists. Now push backward so that your arms are straight again. Repetitions: ten at first; fifteen to twenty optimum. You can make this exercise harder by moving your feet farther away from the object and putting them together. You are doing this exercise properly if you feel it in your shoulders.

arm exercises

29. Book Curls

Stand holding two books of equal weight, one in each hand (palms up), out in front of you. One arm at a time, raise the book up toward your chin slowly and lower back down slowly, alternating arms. Do this five times on each arm at first, working up to fifteen times on each arm. To make this harder, you can use heavier books.

30. Pull-Ups

Pull-ups are good for the biceps muscles of the arms and also the muscles in your shoulders, chest, and back. Do them with your hand in a forward grip and a little farther apart than shoulder width. Pull smoothly up until your chin reaches the bar, then let yourself down until your arms are straight for one repetition. Work up to ten repetitions, and do one to two sets each workout.

31. Triceps Push-Offs

Stand facing a table or other sturdy object that comes up to just below waist height. Place your hands on the table so the heels of your palms are on the edge to push off from. Lean forward, bending elbows downward so that the stress is placed on the upper arms and your head meets your hands. Now push back up to original position to complete the rep. Do five reps at first and work up to twenty for a full set. You should feel this exercise in the triceps muscles at the back of your arms. To make this exercise more difficult, stand farther away from the object with your feet together.

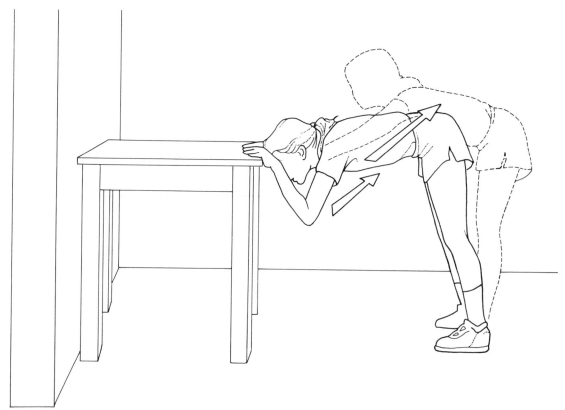

32. Body Dips

This is for the triceps muscles at the rear of the arms. Stand with back to a chair placed against the wall, and place hands behind you on chair's seat. Feet should be placed forward of the body about two to three feet. Lower buttocks down toward the floor until your chest is on a plane with your hands, then raise back up to starting position to complete one repetition. Do this eight to ten times at first, working up to twenty for one set.

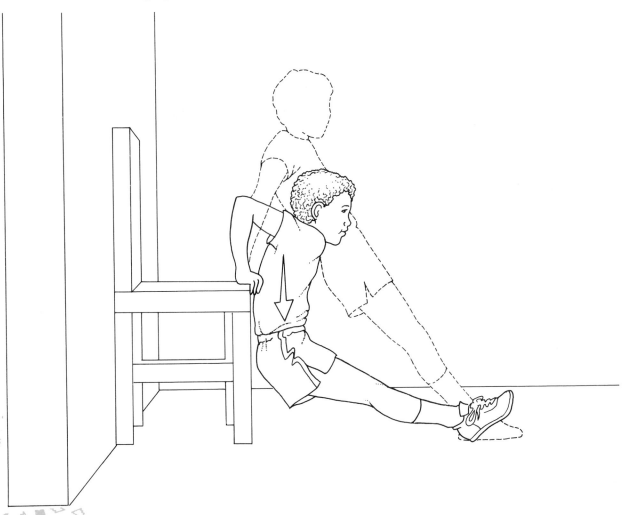

APPENDIX D

skill builders and drills

a. tips

All sports and games that require bodily movement will help develop motor skills, and the more sports and active games you try out in the eleven-to-fourteen age years, the better for your skills development. Following this is a list of a few skill-building activities and drills that most people can do at home alone or with two or three other people. But first, a few tips on how to make the most of your skill-building activities:

▶ Don't worry if you don't do everything perfectly. Kicking a ball and having it go exactly where you want it may be easy for some people and difficult for others—it will vary from person to person, and the object here is to compete against yourself. Try to do better today than you did yesterday, or last week. On a day-to-day basis, the key is progress, not perfection.

▶ I recommend you pick one or two of the drills for each skills workout and try to improve your performance at those for at least two or three workouts before going on to other drills. The point is to *master*, not just try out, as many skills as possible.

▶ You should always do skill drills when you are fresh, not right after some other exercise.

▶ Warm up for and cool down from your skills workouts the same as you do in your aerobic workouts.

▶ Stick with it. Like any other portion of your fitness program, you have to stick with these drills in order to get results.

b. list of skill activities and drills

jumping rope *(whole-body coordination, balance, agility, foot speed):* Jumping rope is great exercise and also a great skill builder. Start with a simple two-foot hop over the rope and then develop other skills—skipping over the rope, jumping on one foot at a time, crossing your arms, etc.

the turning stork *(balance, balance stabilization):* This drill lets you practice stabilizing your body's balance during movement, an important skill in most sports. You should do this in socks on a slick floor. Stand on your right leg with the foot of the left leg braced against the inside of your right thigh, with hands on hips. Stand for five seconds, then swivel on the ball of your foot 180 degrees to your right. After five more seconds of standing, swivel 180 degrees more to your right, back to your original position. Stand for five seconds in that position, then make two 180-degree swivels to your left. When you get to the point where you can do four or five of these rotations to either side, try them with your eyes closed. Now do the same on the left leg.

tire run *(balance, foot speed, multilimb coordination, eye-foot coordination, agility):* Set up old tires in the pattern shown in the illustration, and practice running (slowly at first) through them. Run the course with your left foot going into the tires on your left and your right foot going into the tires on your right. Then run in a normal way (one foot ahead of the other) through one line of tires and back through the other line.

soccer dribble obstacle course (*eye-foot coordination, balance, whole body coordination, agility*): Set up a course like one of the ones shown in the illustration using old tires, milk cartons, and similar things, and practice dribbling a soccer ball through the course with your feet. Vary the dimensions of the course (the closer the objects are to each other, the harder) and experiment with your own course designs.

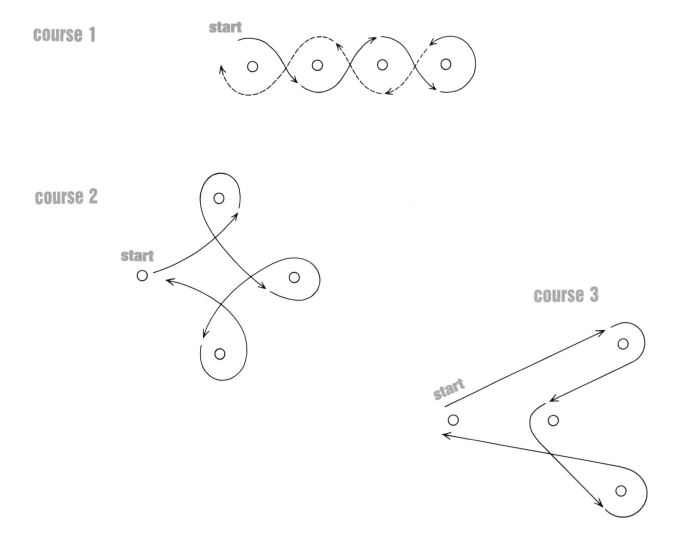

basketball dribble obstacle course (*eye-hand coordination, whole-body coordination, balance, agility, dexterity*): Practice dribbling a basketball through one or more of the courses shown for the soccer dribble, or make up your own course.

bicycle obstacle course *(whole-body coordination, balance, balance stabilization)*: Biking, particularly BMX and off-road mountain biking, is a great skill builder. Make the course shown in the illustration with old tires and practice riding through it both from left to right and from right to left. As you get better at it, move the tires closer together.

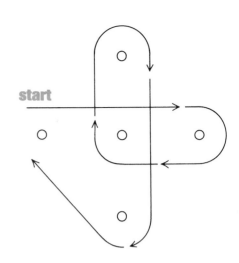

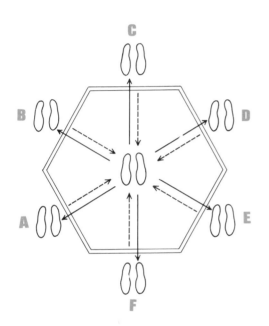

hexagonal jump *(balance, whole-body coordination, agility, foot speed)*: This is one of the best overall skill developers there is, and is used as a test by the Austrian Ski Team to determine alpine skiing ability. With two-inch masking tape, create the hexagon shown in the illustration (twenty-two inches per side) on a hard, flat surface. Stand in the middle of the hex facing side F, as you must for the duration of the drill. Jump out of the hex over side A and immediately back into the hex. Then, continuing to face side F, jump over side B and back into the hex, over side C and back into the hex, over D and back in, over E and back in, and finally over side F and back in for one complete revolution. Your feet should not touch any one of the lines. Practice going around once perfectly, then twice, then three times, as fast as you can. Some top junior alpine skiers can do three complete revolutions without touching a line with their feet in nine seconds. See if you can work down to that!

softball throw *(hand-eye coordination, aim)*: Take a softball and, if you are throwing with your right hand, take one step forward with your left leg and throw the ball at a large target (a tree with a tire swing is great for practicing). If you are throwing with your left hand, take one step forward with your right leg. Start this about fifteen feet from your target and gradually work up to one hundred feet away. Try your best to throw the ball hard and accurately.

The following is a list of works consulted in the research of these books:

COOPER, KENNETH H., M.D. *Kid Fitness: A Complete Shape-Up Program from Birth Through High School.* New York: Bantam, 1991.

American Academy of Pediatrics. *Caring for Your Baby and Child, Birth to Age 5.* Edited by STEVEN P. SHELOV, M.D., F.A.A.P. (editor-in-chief), and ROBERT E. HANNEMANN, M.D., F.A.A.P. (associate medical editor). New York: Bantam, 1991.

ANDERSON, BOB. *Stretching.* Bolinas, Calif.: Shelter Publications, Inc., 1980.

ARNOT, ROBERT, M.D., and CHARLES GAINES. *Sports Talent.* New York: Viking Penguin, 1984.

EISENBERG, ARLENE, HEIDI E. MURKOFF, and SANDEE E. HATHAWAY, B.S.N. *What to Expect the First Year.* New York: Workman, 1989.

FIRKALY, SUSAN TATE. *Into the Mouths of Babes.* White Hall, Va.: Betterway Publications, Inc., 1984.

GAINES, CHARLES, and GEORGE BUTLER. *Staying Hard.* New York: Kenan Press, 1988.

GLOVER, BOB, and JACK SHEPHERD. *The Family Fitness Handbook.* New York: The Penguin Group, 1989.

KUNTZLEMAN, DR. CHARLES T. *Healthy Kids for Life.* New York: Simon and Schuster, 1988.

KUNTZLEMAN, CHARLES, and BETH and MICHAEL and GAIL MCGLYNN. *Aerobics with Fun.* Reston, Va.: AAHPERD, 1991.

LEACH, PENELOPE, Ph.D. *Your Baby & Child from Birth to Age Five.* New York: Alfred A. Knopf, 1990.

MCCOY, KATHY, and CHARLES WIBBELSMAN, M.D. *The New Teenage Body Book.* Los Angeles: The Body Press, 1987.

MCINALLY, PAT. *Moms & Dads, Kids & Sports.* New York: Charles Scribners Sons, 1988.

MICHELI, LYLE J., M.D. *Sportswise: An Essential Guide for Young Athletes, Parents, and Coaches.* Boston: Houghton Mifflin, 1990.

ORLICK, TERRY. *The Cooperative Sports & Games Book.* New York: Pantheon Books, 1978.

PETRAY, DR. CLAYRE K., and SANDRA L. BLAZER. *Health-Related Physical Fitness: Concepts and Activities for Elementary School Children.* Edina, Minn.: Bellwether Press, 1987.

ROWLAND, THOMAS W. *Exercise and Children's Health.* Champaign, Ill.: Human Kinetics Books, 1990.

First and foremost, special thanks to Jane Forrestal Ellsworth. Thanks also to Stephen Lesko, graduate assistant at Springfield College, Springfield, Mass.; Dr. Mimi Murray, Springfield College; Donna Israel, nutrition expert at Cooper Institute; Janice M. O'Donnell, NHAHPERD; Diane Rappa, NHAHPERD; Tom Walton, physical education teacher at Rundlett Junior High School, Concord, N.H.; Professor Vern Seefeldt, Director, Youth Sports Institute, Michigan State University; Suzie Boos, RightStart Program, Children's Hospital of Illinois; Becky Davang, Kids' Aerobics, Sugar Land, Tex.; Susan Astor, President, Playorena, Roslyn Heights, N.Y.; Doug Moss, Marketing Specialist, Gymboree; Doug Curry, President (1991), MHAHPERD (Michigan); Sharon Nicosia, physical education teacher, Beaver Meadow Elementary School, Concord, N.H.; Beth Kirkpatrick, physical education teacher, Tilford Middle School, Vinton, Iowa, and past recipient of the Teacher of the Year Award from AAHPERD; Lani Graham, NASPE (part of AAHPERD); Lyle J. Micheli, M.D., Boston Children's Hospital; Dr. Charles T. Kuntzleman; Jill Werman; Louise McCormick, Plymouth State College, Plymouth, N.H.; President's Council on Physical Fitness and Sports, Washington, D.C.; American Alliance for Health, Physical Education, Recreation and Dance, Reston, Va.; Kenneth Cooper, M.D.; Dan Green; Charles L. Sterling, Ed.D.; Robert Arnot, M.D.; Judy Young, NASPE; Dave Camione, University of Connecticut, Storrs; Hal Jordan, Manchester YMCA, Manchester, N.H.; John Cates, University of California, San Diego; Jackie Aher, illustrator; Michael Palgon, Editor, Bantam Doubleday Dell; David Seybold; Jillian Neal, My Gym, Santa Monica, Calif.; Betty Glass, Santa Monica Alternative Schoolhouse, Santa Monica, Calif.

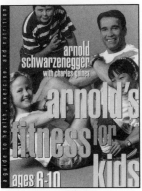